⟜ Praise for Emotionally Intelligent Leadership for Students: Workbook

"The best leaders know and understand themselves, and this includes their emotional intelligence. This book will be a 'must' in my tool kit as I work with future leaders in helping them realize their potential."

—*Kelly Jo Karnes, Office of Student Life,*
associate director, University of Iowa

"As a college administrator who has been intimately involved with student leadership development for the past thirty years, I find the *Emotionally Intelligent Leadership for Students: Workbook* to be an excellent resource. This is a publication for your office shelf that can be referenced at a glance. When a leadership topic requires your attention, you will find many useful components in this workbook to support your educational efforts, including activities, student quotes, and additional resources, along with learning objectives to align your goals and outcomes!"

—*Pamela Brewer, associate dean of students,*
director of student life programs, Lafayette College

"Whether you work with student organization leaders, train residence assistants or supervise student employees, you will find the *Emotionally Intelligent Leadership for Students: Workbook* valuable. The modules offer practical ways of demonstrating theory, and the case studies give students helpful, true-to-life problems to solve and discuss. I look forward to using it with my advanced leadership programs."

—*Kim Roeder, director of student activities,*
Christopher Newport University

"I am excited to have this new resource for illustrating leadership concepts from the follower's perspective. I can't wait to use these exercises in my leadership class."

—Adam Peck, Ph.D., *dean of student affairs,*
Stephen F. Austin State University

Emotionally Intelligent Leadership for Students

Workbook

Marcy Levy Shankman and Scott J. Allen

Editors

JB JOSSEY-BASS™
STUDENT LEADERSHIP

CONTENTS

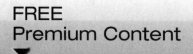

FREE
Premium Content

JOSSEY-BASS™
An Imprint of
WILEY

This book includes premium content that can be
accessed from our Web site when you register at
www.josseybass.com/go/shankman
using the password josseybasshighereducation.

PREFACE

When we sat down to write the book *Emotionally Intelligent Leadership: A Guide for College Students*, we began by discussing the purpose of the book. Although some authors may come to a project with different goals, we came with a shared vision. We intended to write the book as a vehicle for sharing our ideas with as broad an audience as possible. We wanted to introduce emotionally intelligent leadership (EIL) to students, professionals working with students, faculty, and others who engage with students throughout their college experience.

Regardless of your role (student, administrator, faculty, staff), we believe this subject has the potential to make a difference in student leadership development. For students, EIL provides a lens to view themselves and enhance their capacity to make a difference on campus and in their community. For those working with students, EIL provides a framework for supervision, advising, teaching, mentoring, coaching—the application potential is wide open.

In some ways, we think about EIL as the baseball diamond in the movie *Field of Dreams*—"If you build it, they will come." Leadership is available to all of us—and to all students who desire to enhance their skills. Student organizations, residence halls, project teams, workplaces, the larger campus community— all are potential practice fields for those interested in making a difference in the lives of others. And we think EIL provides students with one way to embark on a future full of amazing possibilities.

So here we are, on the next step of our journey—and, we hope, of yours. From the outset, even while we were writing the book, we envisioned a suite of EIL resources. These resources provide direct, hands-on learning experiences for students and professionals alike. The suite consists of five separate but inter-related resources:

- *Emotionally Intelligent Leadership: A Guide for College Students*
- *Emotionally Intelligent Leadership for Students: Inventory*
- *Emotionally Intelligent Leadership for Students: Facilitation and Activity Guide*
- *Emotionally Intelligent Leadership for Students: Student Workbook*
- *Emotionally Intelligent Leadership for Students: Development Guide*

⤺ Emotionally Intelligent Leadership: A Guide for College Students

Emotionally Intelligent Leadership: A Guide for College Students is a groundbreaking book that combines the concepts of emotional intelligence (EI) and leadership in one model: emotionally intelligent leadership (EIL). This important resource offers students a practical guide for developing their EIL capacities and emphasizes that leadership is a learnable skill that is based on developing healthy and effective relationships. Step by step, we outline the EIL model of three facets (consciousness of context, consciousness of self, and consciousness of others) and explore the twenty-one capacities that define emotionally intelligent leadership.

⤺ The Inventory

One of the greatest challenges in leadership development is translating theory into practice—how do the big ideas about leadership make sense to us as individuals so that we can behave differently? Talking about leadership is one thing—integrating ideas about leadership into our thoughts and actions is another.

Assessments serve many purposes along this line—making an abstract concept real, translating theory into practice, and finding meaningful connections between ideas and ourselves. The *Inventory* is our contribution to the field of assessment.

The *Inventory* offers a formative learning experience. While some leadership assessments are diagnostic or predictive in nature, the *Inventory* is an opportunity for individuals to explore their experiences in leadership with a focus on learning one's strengths and limitations based on past behaviors. At the same time, the *Inventory* propels students' thinking into the future with a focus on self-improvement and leadership development. Results include an enhanced understanding of EIL and its application, identification of perceived strengths and limitations, and a determination of direction for leadership development.

A free downloadable *Inventory Facilitator's Guide* is available (see page x); it also appears as an appendix to the *Facilitation and Activity Guide*.

✦ The Facilitation and Activity Guide

The *Facilitation and Activity Guide* is written for leadership educators and practitioners, campus-based professionals, faculty, and anyone interested in guiding students through hands-on learning opportunities that deepen their understanding of emotionally intelligent leadership. The *Facilitation and Activity Guide* is organized in a similar fashion to *Emotionally Intelligent Leadership: A Guide for College Students*, with at least one chapter (module) dedicated to each of the three facets (consciousness of context, consciousness of self, consciousness of others) and the twenty-one capacities of EIL. Each module provides everything that a facilitator needs to know to prepare and facilitate the learning experience (generally forty-five to sixty minutes in length). The modules are written with specific directions, talking points, and discussion questions. When supplemental materials are needed, they are listed at the outset. This resource includes the worksheets, also found in the *Student Workbook*, that the students may utilize during the course of the learning experience. Finally, the *Facilitation and Activity Guide* includes a facilitation plan, suggested program designs, and syllabi in the appendices.

The Student Workbook

Recognizing the need for students to actively engage in their learning, the *Student Workbook* supports and complements the material covered in the *Facilitation and Activity Guide* and the *Inventory*. The *Student Workbook* includes handouts, learning activities, case studies, questions for reflection, and additional resources for further learning. Each chapter of the *Student Workbook* follows the flow of *Emotionally Intelligent Leadership: A Guide for College Students* and the *Facilitation and Activity Guide*. Students may also use the *Student Workbook* as a follow-up to the *EIL Inventory*.

The Development Guide

The *Development Guide* provides students with hundreds of ideas for improvement. The *Development Guide* offers the reader a description of each capacity and a picture of what it looks like to others when an individual is over- or underusing each capacity. In addition, we identify dozens of films, online resources, learning opportunities, books, student quotes, and reflection questions for each of the twenty-one capacities. An individual interested in developing these skills will find a strong foundation in the material and the guidance needed to begin this work.

Eleanor Roosevelt said "living and learning go hand in hand" (Gerber, 2002, p. 256). We believe that this notion extends to leadership—we all have the potential to lead. It's up to us to do it. We hope these resources help students further discover the leadership potential within them. And we hope these materials empower those working with students—to help them guide students in their development, and perhaps, along the way, learn more about their own leadership. We certainly have.

Marcy Levy Shankman, Ph.D.

Scott J. Allen, Ph.D.

REFERENCE

Gerber, R. (2002). *Leadership the Eleanor Roosevelt way: Timeless strategies from the first lady of courage.* New York: Portfolio.

ACKNOWLEDGMENTS

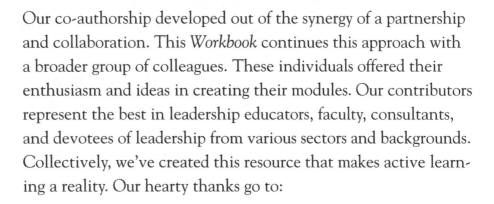

Our co-authorship developed out of the synergy of a partnership and collaboration. This *Workbook* continues this approach with a broader group of colleagues. These individuals offered their enthusiasm and ideas in creating their modules. Our contributors represent the best in leadership educators, faculty, consultants, and devotees of leadership from various sectors and backgrounds. Collectively, we've created this resource that makes active learning a reality. Our hearty thanks go to:

Ginny Carroll, principal, inGINuity

Les Cook, Ed.D., vice president for student affairs, Michigan Technological University

Lucy Shaffer Croft, Ed.D., assistant vice president for student affairs, University of North Florida

Jon Dooley, Ph.D., senior associate dean of student development, Marquette University

Tara Edberg, assistant director for leadership programs, The University of Iowa

Darin Eich, Ph.D., leadership facilitator and consultant, ProgramInnovation.com and CollegeMotivation.com

Paige Haber, instructor, Department of Leadership Studies, University of San Diego

Mike Hayes, executive director of campus life, Washington University in St. Louis

Amy Kautz, coordinator for resident student learning, University of South Carolina

Gabrielle Lucke, director, Training and Educational Programs, Office of Institutional Diversity and Equity, Dartmouth College

Gary Manka, director for student government advising, training and operations, University of South Florida

Jim Meehan, law student, University of Akron

Anthony Middlebrooks, Ph.D., assistant professor, Organizational and Community Leadership, School of Urban Affairs and Public Policy University of Delaware

Susana Muñoz, Ph.D., postdoctoral research associate, Department of Educational Leadership & Policy Studies, Iowa State University

Cathy Onion, assistant professor, Western Illinois University

Adam Peck, Ph.D., dean of student affairs, Stephen F. Austin State University

Mary Peterson, executive director, Sigma Lambda Gamma and Sigma Lambda Beta

Tracy Purinton, associate director, MIT Leadership Center

Darbi Roberts, student development coordinator, Carnegie Mellon University in Qatar

Sabrina Ryan, coordinator of Greek programs, Case Western Reserve University

Wes Schaub, director of Greek life, Case Western Reserve University

John Shertzer, vice president, Leadership Ventures

Karyn Nishimura Sneath, owner, nPower

Sarah Spengler, principal, Grace Partners, LLC

Diana Wilson, advanced program coordinator, Center for Early Childhood Studies, Pima Community College/University of Arizona Undergraduate Community of Practice

We also appreciate the contributions from students in Scott's summer 2009 course in leadership and management skills:

Will Bargar

Bryan Gacka

Amy Gourniak

Mark Greisberger

Veronika Julia Korner

Andrea Kovacs

Paul Martin

Eric Megla

Kristyn Riemer

Jessica Sindelar

John Smith

Mike Spinelli

Josh Merkle contributed his thoughtful comments in review of this work.

We are indebted to our wonderful editor, Erin Null. She has been an important partner in developing these materials with guidance and continued enthusiasm. Each time we bring a creative or crazy idea to her, she responds with clarity and thoughtfulness.

Finally, we are thankful we both have families that are patient and always supportive—they keep us grounded, and without them, who knows where we'd be?

ABOUT THE AUTHORS

Marcy Levy Shankman, Ph.D., has been training and consulting in leadership development and organizational effectiveness since 1998. She is principal of MLS Consulting LLC, which she founded in 2001, and enjoys working with a wide range of clients, from small direct service agencies to national voluntary associations, from local high schools to large public universities. Marcy facilitates strategic planning and visioning initiatives, organizational change and development projects, as well as leadership training and coaching. Marcy has spoken to various groups in the local nonprofit community as well as conferences and campuses across the country. Her focus is on helping students, young and experienced professionals, faculty, and staff to consider ways to enhance their own leadership development.

Marcy also teaches as a Presidential Fellow for the SAGES program of Case Western Reserve University and as an instructor in the David Brain Leadership Program of Baldwin-Wallace College. Prior to establishing her training and consulting practice, Marcy held professional positions with the Indiana University Center on Philanthropy, the Hillel Foundation at the George Washington University, and the Office of Orientation Services at the University of Iowa.

Marcy actively volunteers with her alma mater, The College of William and Mary, her local school district, the learning committee of her synagogue, and the Organizational Assessment Committee of the United Way of Greater Cleveland.

Marcy lives in Shaker Heights, Ohio, with her husband and two children.

Scott J. Allen, Ph.D., is an assistant professor of management at John Carroll University, where he teaches leadership and management skills. In 2005, Scott developed the Center for Leader Development (www.centerforleaderdevelopment. com), a blog that explores the study and practice of leadership development.

Scott is published in the *Encyclopedia of Leadership* and completed a chapter for the China Executive Leadership Academy Pudong, entitled "A Review on Leadership Education and Development Outside China." He is also a contributing author of the book *Leadership: The Key Concepts* (Routledge, 2007). In addition, his work is featured in a number of academic journals, such as the *Journal of Leadership Educators*, *Advances in Developing Human Resources*, *Leadership Review*, *The OD Journal*, *SAM Advanced Management Journal*, *International Leadership Journal*, *Journal of Leadership Studies*, and *Leadership Excellence*.

In addition to his writing and work in the classroom, Scott consults, facilitates workshops, and leads retreats across industries. Scott is involved in the International Leadership Association and serves on the board of trustees of Beta Theta Pi Fraternity. Since 2007, he has served as a Sam Walton Fellow for Students in Free Enterprise (SIFE).

Scott resides in Chagrin Falls, Ohio, with his wife and three children.

INTRODUCTION

Most, if not all of us, have been told at some time in our lives that "practice makes perfect." Although we don't buy into the ideal of perfection ourselves, we do believe that practice is essential. Developing the discipline of practice is familiar to many—artists, athletes, scientists, and others who pursue professional excellence. In our fast-moving, ever-changing world, however, we worry that we're losing the commitment to practice. As technology improves and experiences and activities become more accessible to more of us, it almost seems that an expectation of mastery has emerged alongside this trend towards greater access. Unfortunately, for anyone interested in developing leadership skills, an expectation of immediate mastery is a dangerous assumption. Leadership, like many other complex activities, requires practice to master.

We created this workbook as a vehicle for those interested in developing their leadership capacity. The model of emotionally intelligent leadership rests on the premise that leadership is available to all of us—no one is born a leader, and leadership does not require a position or a title. Leadership occurs all around us, and we can choose to jump into the fray or stand by and watch the action. What leadership requires, however, is intentionality. This workbook provides a variety of learning experiences to the reader, all of which are designed to support the development of specific leadership abilities.

Emotionally Intelligent Leadership: A Brief Overview

Emotionally intelligent leadership (EIL) synthesizes two major bodies of research and theory: emotional intelligence and leadership. In 1990, Peter Salovey and John Mayer published a paper in which they coined the term *emotional intelligence*.

They defined EI as "the ability to monitor one's own and others emotions, to use the information to guide one's thinking and actions" (p. 189). Goleman (1998) added that emotional intelligence is "the capacity for recognizing our own feelings and those of others, for motivating ourselves, and for managing emotions well in ourselves and in our relationships" (p. 317).

Integrating leadership scholarship and research led us to conclude that the leader must demonstrate consciousness of self, consciousness of others, and consciousness of context. These *facets* of emotionally intelligent leadership are central to whether effective (or ineffective) leadership is demonstrated. A person's skill in monitoring all three facets intentionally will aid in the person's ability to lead well. After all, leaders, whether informal or formal, must be aware of their own capacities, the needs of those who follow or work with them, and the environmental factors that come into play.

EIL also consists of twenty-one capacities to which a person should pay attention; these are grouped under the three facets: consciousness of context, self, and others (see Box 1.1). The word *capacity* is defined as "ability to perform or produce; capability." (All dictionary definitions in this EIL series are from the *American Heritage Dictionary*.) We chose this word because, as noted, we all have the capacity to develop the ability to lead others effectively.

✦ Using This Workbook

This book is designed to be a "working" book. We want you to write in it, fold pages, complete a page and then, sometime later, come back to it and use it as you engage in other leadership opportunities. The book contains a variety of hands-on learning experiences that provide you with different ways to learn more about the three facets and twenty-one capacities of EIL. Each

Box 1.1. Emotionally Intelligent Leadership

Consciousness of context
The environment in which leaders and followers work

Environmental awareness
Thinking intentionally about the environment of a leadership situation

Group savvy
Interpreting the situation and/or networks of an organization

Consciousness of self
Being aware of yourself in terms of your abilities and emotions

Emotional self-perception
Identifying your emotions and reactions and their impact on you

Honest self-understanding
Being aware of your own strengths and limitations

Healthy self-esteem
Having a balanced sense of self

Emotional self-control
Consciously moderating your emotions and reactions

Authenticity
Being transparent and trustworthy

Flexibility
Being open and adaptive to changing situations

Achievement
Being driven to improve according to personal standards

(Continued)

Optimism
Being positive

Initiative
Wanting and seeking opportunities

Consciousness of others
Being aware of your relationship with others and the role they play in
   the leadership equation

Empathy
Understanding others from their perspective

Citizenship
Recognizing and fulfilling your responsibility for others or the group

Inspiration
Motivating and moving others toward a shared vision

Influence
Demonstrating skills of persuasion

Coaching
Helping others enhance their skills and abilities

Change agent
Seeking and working with others toward new directions

Conflict management
Identifying and resolving problems with others

Developing relationships
Creating connections between, among, and with people

Teamwork
Working effectively with others in a group

Capitalizing on difference
Building on assets that come from differences with others

chapter has at least one exercise or worksheet, quotes by students on the subject, and a list of resources for additional learning. Many chapters also include a case study.

We encourage you to use this book in the way that makes the most sense to you. If you've already read the book *Emotionally Intelligent Leadership: A Guide for College Students*, then you probably know what you want to learn more about. If you haven't, that's fine too; re-read the model on the previous page and go to the facet or capacity that most interests you. Perhaps you've taken the *Emotionally Intelligent Leadership for Students: Inventory* and want to use this book as a way to continue the learning. In that case, start with the theme you identified as your primary area of interest for further development. If you're attending a workshop or class on a topic that is presented here, then your facilitator will guide you to where to go based on the activities of the session. If you're picking up this book on your own, feel free to go through the book in the order in which the activities and ideas are presented, or skip around to the capacities and facets that most interest you. You can explore this workbook and use it in the ways that make the most sense to you.

What matters most is that you begin the work. Take the first step. If you've already done that, now it's time to take a bigger step. A popular cliché in the field of leadership development is that leadership is a lifelong journey. For some, this phrase resonates with their life experiences, and they know what they want their journey to look like. For others, the phrase may sound hollow. What we know, from both research and personal experience, is that developing your leadership potential and honing your practice of leadership takes time and effort. It takes work. We hope that this workbook helps you on your own path and leads you in the direction of creating meaningful change for you and those around you.

Marcy Levy Shankman, Ph.D.
Scott J. Allen, Ph.D.

REFERENCES

Goleman, D. (1998). *Working with emotional intelligence*. New York: Bantam Books.

Salovey, P., & Mayer, J. D. (1990). Emotional intelligence. *Imagination, Cognition, and Personality*, 9(3), 185–211.

Consciousness of Context

Focus

Consciousness of context means thinking intentionally about the environment of a leadership situation. The larger system, or environment, has notable influence on an individual's ability to lead. Similarly, the situation and setting in which leadership occurs are important factors for consideration. Aspects of the environment directly affect the psychological and interpersonal dynamics of any human interaction. Being conscious of the context entails recognizing a variety of environmental factors such as community traditions and customs, the political environment, and even small group dynamics.

Learning Objectives

- To explore what consciousness of context means
- To learn about how the physical environment influences a leadership opportunity
- To learn how to identify key internal and external factors that may influence leadership

Consciousness of Context
Module 1, Activity 1: Identifying Context

By Marcy Levy Shankman and Scott J. Allen

Concentric Circles

As suggested in the example below, fill in the rings of the blank circle with the different dimensions of context for a group (formal or informal) that is familiar to you. This could be an organization in which you're a member or leader or even a friendship group. How many more rings can you add to the circle?

Example:

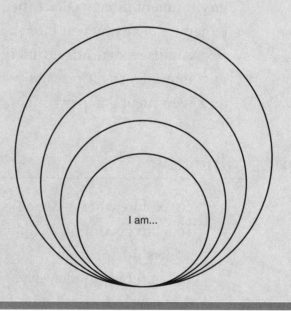

Consciousness of Context
Module 1, Activity 2: Context Fieldtrip

By Marcy Levy Shankman and Scott J. Allen

Completing the following chart will help you better understand the different contexts that you experience. Throughout the course of a day or a week, complete the chart, reflecting the groups or organizations to which you belong and the factors that influence them. Each group or organization should be considered in light of its particular setting and situation. The more you begin to see the layers of influence, the more attuned you will become to seeing the role that context plays in exercising leadership. Remember to consider informal groups that you're a part of like a group of friends or those with whom you live or regularly interact (like a class).

A few questions to consider:

Setting:

- What is the internal structure of the group?
- How is it organized?
- What formal positions and/or committees exist?
- What larger group or entity includes your group or organization?
- What are the set expectations or rules for operating?
- What is the physical location in which the group or organization operates?

Situation:

- What is happening at present?
- What are the internal challenges?
- Where is the focus of energy for the group?
- What outside factors are influencing decisions that are being made?
- What outside factors are causing stress?
- What opportunities exist because of the current situation?

(Continued)

Group or Organization	Setting	Situation

Consciousness of Context
Module 1, Activity 3: Reflection

By Marcy Levy Shankman and Scott J. Allen

Consider the following student quotes about how context relates to leadership.

When external forces make a team's work seem more relevant, it's easier to inspire group members and feel as though I'm impacting what is happening in a positive manner.

The environment has a large impact on how effectively a group can operate. If a group is willing to participate and has a high energy level, then I feel more compelled to have a similar attitude. If a group doesn't show interest, though, it sometimes seems better just to give up.

Environment can either make or break leadership ability. If you are working around others in an environment where they fully support your duties, you will succeed many times over. If you are constantly battling for credibility, it will start to feel troublesome or hopeless.

I feel that sometimes the environment is one that you create, and sometimes it is created by others. If I am placed in a position to lead, I would hope that it would be one where everyone's ideas can be expressed.

The environment describes the mood, almost what I want to call the "integrity" of the organization or group. If it's a positive

(Continued)

environment, that's great, but when it lacks support and communication, there is room for error and even failure.

If you are in an environment that is hostile or work with people you don't get along with, then you can't focus on your work and as a result your organization's efficiency suffers. Also, an environment where you do not get feedback from your superiors leaves you wondering if you are doing a good job. Effective communication, supportive or critical, is essential.

Reflection questions

1. Which quote makes the most sense to you? Why?

2. Which quote do you think is the most controversial? Why?

3. Based on these observations, what might you consider doing differently the next time you have the opportunity to lead?

✦ Student Quotes

My environment influences and affects my ability to lead my organization, groups, or teams in a major way. The factors of an emotionally safe and welcoming environment are weighted much more heavily for me when dealing with my different organizations and groups. Establishing a healthy working environment is crucial for creating a synergistic team.

I think there is a level of comfort associated with every environment. That level of comfort, whether comfortable or uncomfortable, leads to differences in how I can lead. The environment plays a factor when it comes to space, resources, and outside factors that may distract or aggravate the group. The environment either acts as a catalyst or deterrent for everything you do.

An environment that I feel comfortable in is a huge factor on my ability to lead. If I feel that I am in the kind of place where I can say what I want and take charge, then I am more likely to lead. However, if a teacher, advisor, or another student is imposing or not inviting, I often have the feeling that I want to just sit back and not be noticed.

I believe it is beneficial for groups to operate in a variety of environments. This could mean having meetings or events in different places, varying how organizations interact, etc.

ADDITIONAL RESOURCES

Pink, D. H. (2005). *A whole new mind: Moving from the information age to the conceptual age*. New York: Riverhead Books.

Schein, E. H. (1992). *Organizational culture and leadership*, 3rd ed. San Francisco: Jossey-Bass.

Senge, P. (1990). *The fifth discipline: The art and practice of the learning organization*. New York: Doubleday.

Wheatley, M. J. (1992). *Leadership and the new science: Learning about organization from an orderly universe*. San Francisco: Berrett-Koehler.

2

Environmental Awareness

✦ Focus

Environmental awareness entails thinking intentionally about
the environment of a leadership situation. The larger system,
or environment, directly influences an individual's ability to
lead. Aspects of the environment affect the psychological and
interpersonal dynamics of any human interaction. Emotionally
intelligent leaders are in tune with a variety of factors such
as community traditions and customs, the political environment, and major institutions (e.g., religion, government).
Demonstrating environmental awareness means having the
ability to observe these dynamics and factors present in
the environment as they occur. Being aware of one's environment enables a person to use this knowledge to determine a
course of action with greater perspective and insight.

✦ Learning Objectives

- To increase awareness about the full range of decision
  options available when thinking about the future

- To realize how time plays a role in decision making
- To identify desired future goals
- To explore the implications of how your environment influences choices and potential future decisions

Environmental Awareness
Module 2, Activity 1: Strung-Out Decisions

By Anthony Middlebrooks

Emotionally intelligent leadership includes being aware of your context, in the present and the future. Having a greater understanding of where actions will lead to in the future enables you to more effectively influence others toward a vision. Understanding the full array of options for action reveals the broad spectrum of relevant emotions, in both yourself and others. Consider your own context, specific decisions you face, and the relevant emotions that each decision option entails.

1. Identify an important decision that you are currently facing:

2. For the decision you identify in item #1, brainstorm as many decision options as possible. Determine when that particular decision option will or may expire; for example, at what point will it be too late to pursue that option? Fill in your decision options in accordance with the relevant time frame noted and describe the emotions you feel in relation to each decision option.

(Continued)

Decision options: **How you feel:**

Now or never:

Ending next month:

Ending next year:

In five years:

In ten years:

Never ending . . .

3. Share your ideas with another person and together brainstorm
    five to ten more decision options. Challenge yourself to move
    beyond the most obvious decision options to see the full array,
    even if some of those options appear impractical at first glance.

✦ Student Quotes

When external forces make a team's work seem more relevant, it's a lot easier to inspire group members and feel as though I'm impacting the team in a positive manner.

If you are in an environment that is hostile or work with people you don't get along with, then you can't focus on your work and as a result your organization's efficiency suffers.

I think that the environmental impacts are dually faceted. The first facet is the staff/administration/advisors. They can play a big role, and whether or not they like it, they can have a lot of influence over students. Their attitudes and opinions will mold the behavior of a group. The other facet is the nature [of the] host institution. In a school where the majority of students are supported in their endeavors, you will see more successful leaders. A school that does not encourage student-run programming will have a negative effect on student life.

The environment must be professional . . . and equitable. A professional environment helps to maintain a more serious tone. . . . An equitable environment helps each member feel they are of value.

The environment has a total effect on how I lead. I am a better leader in a positive environment rather than a negative environment.

The environment, and especially the attitudes of those people you lead within an organization, affect your ability to lead. To foster change within an organization, it is critical to first get buy-in from the individuals whose behaviors or attitudes will be changed. Without this, change will be difficult.

ADDITIONAL RESOURCES

Books

Banyai, I. (1998). *Zoom*. New York: Puffin.

Banyai, I. (1998). *Re-Zoom*. New York: Puffin.

Bergquist, W. H., & Pawlak, K. (2008). *Engaging the six cultures of the academy*. San Francisco: Jossey-Bass.

Kuh, J., Schuh, J. H., Whitt, E. J., Andreas, R. E., Lyons, J. W., Strange, C. C., Krehbiel, L. E., & MacKay, K. A. (1991). *Involving colleges: Successful approaches to fostering student learning and development outside the classroom*. San Francisco: Jossey-Bass.

Movies

The Matrix (1999)

Powers of Ten (2000)

The Pursuit of Happyness (2007)

3

Group Savvy

☚ Focus

Group savvy is about interpreting the situation and/or networks of an organization. Every group has written and unwritten rules, ways of operating, customs and rituals, power dynamics, internal politics, inherent values, and so forth. Emotionally intelligent leaders know how to diagnose and interpret these dynamics. Demonstrating group savvy enables one to have a direct influence on the work of the group.

☚ Learning Objectives

- To explore the definition and dynamics of group savvy
- To practice the skills of identifying key elements of a group's culture
- To reflect on experiences of group dynamics and the difficulties involved with learning how to fit in
- To enhance your understanding of how to demonstrate group savvy through analysis, organizational awareness, and asking questions

Group Savvy
Module 3, Activity 1: Diagnosing Organizational Culture

By Ginny Carroll

Learning to recognize and understand an organization from Driskill and Brenton's (2005) *four categories of elements of group culture* will enhance your ability to diagnose what's affecting the culture of a group.

Choose an organization that you belong to and record your answers to the following questions.

Name of organization:

_____

1. What are the symbolic elements? Aspects that represent something of value: logos, web pages, mission statement, organizational stories, slang used by members, formal speeches, and so on. Describe these for your organization:

2. What are the role elements? The two main roles that help in understanding a group's culture: the heroes (people within the organization whom everyone admires) and the villains (members who work against the grain). Who fills these roles for your organization?

3. What are the interactive elements? The rituals, group norms (written/unwritten rules), accepted behaviors, and communication styles demonstrated by groups members and by the group itself. Describe these for your organization:

4. What are the context elements? The important role that place and time play in an organization. An organization's culture is affected by its history, location, and space (both physical space and the context in which the organization exists in relation to its external environment). Describe these for your organization:

Reference

Driskill, G., & Brenton, A. L. (2005). *Organizational culture in action: A cultural analysis workbook.* Thousand Oaks, CA: Sage.

Group Savvy
Module 3, Activity 2: Organizational Awareness
—Reading Social and Political Currents

By Ginny Carroll

People who excel at the capacity of group savvy pay attention to:

Political Savvy

"The ability to read political realities is vital to the behind-the-scenes networking and coalition building that allows someone to wield influence—no matter what their role" (Goleman, 1998, p. 160).

The Invisible Nervous System

"Every organization has its own invisible nervous system of connection and influence" (Goleman, 1998, p. 160). Some people are oblivious to this, whereas others have it fully on their radar screens.

Personal Bias

Understanding the influence of one's own assumptions and knowing how to objectively read situations is a distinguishing skill of organizational awareness. Minimizing the distortions based on personal biases allows people to respond more effectively.

Organizational Climate

Empathizing at the organizational level means being attuned to the climate and culture of the organization. "The inevitable politics of organization life creates competing coalitions and power struggles" (Goleman, 1998, p. 162). Understanding this dynamic and identifying relevant underlying issues enables one to better address what really matters to decision makers.

Disdain or Disinterest

A lack of interest in or disdain for organizational politics is a liability. Those "who lack political astuteness more often blunder in, trying to mobilize others to their cause because their attempts at influence are misdirected or inept" (Goleman, 1998, p. 162).

Political Animals

Some people thrive on organizational politics. Their primary focus is pursuing their own interests and goals. They study "the invisible web of power" (Goleman, 1998, p. 162). Political animals are weakened by their self-interest and tend to ignore information that might be useful to them, thus creating blind spots.

How do each of these manifest themselves in your organization(s)? Which ones are you in tune with, and where could you improve?

Reference

Goleman, D. (1998). *Working with emotional intelligence.* New York: Bantam Books.

Group Savvy
Module 4: Group Savvy, A Summary

By Jim Meehan

How does the capacity of group savvy fit into the larger picture of EIL?

Group savvy is a capacity of consciousness of context, along with environmental awareness. Although closely related to environmental awareness, group savvy focuses on the deeper levels of context in a group, such as the ways the internal politics of an organization affect decisions.

What are the primary characteristics involved in demonstrating group savvy?

Although there are several components of group savvy, reading between the lines, identifying the power players in a group, and knowing how to be an effective member without being told what to do are some of the most important ones.

Why is group savvy an essential capacity of EIL?

Identifying the underlying forces guiding an association of people can enhance your ability to make informed decisions within it. This greater knowledge of the dynamics and inner workings will likely improve your chances of, and effectiveness in, contributing to the group.

What are the critical components of group savvy?

Driskill and Brenton (2005) identify four categories of elements that help you demonstrate group savvy:

Symbolic elements: Those representing the larger values of a group such as its web page and the slang used by members

Role elements: Those that differentiate between the group's heroes (those whom many admire) and its villains (those whom most see as the rebels)

Interactive elements: The behaviors of the group, like ritual and communication styles, that will reveal broader meanings upon further group savvy analysis

Context elements: Those that define the environment and the purpose of the group, such as its physical space and its shared visions

When should one rely on group savvy?

Ideally, group savvy will produce the greatest benefits as you gain experience within a group. Therefore, group savvy might best be acquired and employed on a gradual basis, helping you to navigate your journey toward finding a niche in the group. Asking relevant questions facilitates one's use of group savvy.

References

Driskill, G., & Brenton, A. L. (2005). *Organizational culture in action: A cultural analysis workbook.* Thousand Oaks, CA: Sage.

Shankman, M. L., & Allen, S. J. (2008). *Emotionally intelligent leadership: A guide for college students.* San Francisco: Jossey-Bass.

Group Savvy
Module 4, Activity 3: Group Savvy at the Movies

By Jim Meehan

Identify a movie that you think exemplifies the capacity of group savvy. Using Driskill and Brenton's (2005) elements as a guide, answer the following:

Give a brief explanation of the plot or the context surrounding the use of group savvy in the film.

What did the character(s) do that reflected group savvy and led to his or her acceptance (or lack thereof) in a new organization/group?

What could this character have done differently to better demonstrate the capacity of group savvy?

How was group savvy directly or indirectly related to the character's experiences?

✦ Case Study: Deadlines at InterActiveX

Eric Megla, MBA student

InterActive X is a relatively young company that develops iPhone applications. Bureaucracy and required procedures are minimal. The management style of the company tends to be reactive rather than proactive, and there is no investment in long-term strategy. A few years ago, when the company went public, the forecast for potential growth was extremely positive. However, as a result of the recent recession, sales have been down. Management has communicated to everyone in the company the need to "buckle down" and achieve successful results.

InterActive X has multiple small teams that each "own" an application to develop and improve. One of those teams, team Alpha Dog, has five members: Steve G., Marty, Janet, Adrian, and Molly.

Steve G. recently became the leader of the Alpha Dog team, replacing Jim, who left to work for a competitor. Steve G. is seen as an up-and-comer who is extremely productive and is often called a "technical wizard."

Marty is in his early fifties and has many years of experience in development. He is dependable, but has shown little willingness to lead. Instead, he prefers to stay in his office and complete tasks assigned to him. Marty also tends to do just enough to get a project done without any extra effort. This may be because he secretly believes that extra effort is beneath him and that his many years of experience make him invaluable to the team and company.

Janet, a single mother of two, comes across as friendly to everyone who meets her. She is highly dedicated, but due to family circumstances has trouble working more than forty hours a week.

Adrian reminds others of a young Steve G., as their work habits are similar. Neither Adrian nor Steve G. have families, and both work long hours to get work done. However, at times Adrian's passion can make him appear overbearing, and this has sometimes made others on the team nervous when they've had disagreements with him.

Molly is the youngest team member; a recent college graduate, she has been with InterActive X for less than two years. She is naturally gregarious, and some feel she spends too much time socializing at the office. Molly also takes advantage of other people's talents and good nature. She is often perceived as lazy by people who know her well.

After Steve G. took the helm of the team, he realized that achieving project completion by the release date was unlikely. This was complicated by Jim's previous communications to upper management that the project was on schedule and the group might even release early.

Steve G. hinted that there might be an issue with completing the project by the release date, and his manager, Paul, said he understood that the team's transition had cost time and there had also been a reduction in the workforce. On the other hand, Steve G.'s manager pointed out how successful Steve G. had been in the past and that "times were tough." Paul was willing to allow for a small time extension, perhaps a few days, but more would be impossible.

As a new manager, Steve G. felt compelled to complete the project on time to prove himself. He looked at the schedule and times for the tasks yet to be completed. Steve G. determined that if he asked everyone to work an extra fifteen hours a week for the next few months, and no further delays or issues arose, the project could be completed on time.

Steve G. sent a meeting invitation to team Alpha Dog and indicated that attendance was mandatory. After Marty,

Adrian, Janet, and Molly sat down, Steve G. stood and smiled. "Everyone, I have some good news. After looking at the schedule for release of our new software I see no reason that we cannot release on time."

The team members felt a sigh of relief. With the bad economic times, they were all worried about potential layoffs. Steve G. projected the modified schedule with the increased hours up on the screen, still smiling and impressed with his self-perceived leadership skills. Steve G. did not bother to look at his audience as he explained the need for everyone to work extra hours. He indicated that if any problems occurred during the remainder of the project, he would have to be notified immediately, as there was little room for error.

Had Steve G. looked at his audience, he might have noticed subtle cues that indicated a lack of enthusiasm for this new initiative. Marty, figuring he was not really expected to work any additional hours due to his stature, was less concerned than the others. He just stared out the window, uninterested in the meeting. Janet's face may have shown the most concern. She really could not afford to be at the office any more than she already was, usually just over forty hours a week. She had her two children attending day care after school, occasionally filling in with a babysitter when there were gaps. However, she needed the job and did not want to take any chances during the recession.

Adrian was irritated because he had already been working long hours for the past few months and felt that he had nothing to show for it. He was looking forward to spending less time at the office now that the weather was nice. Molly was concerned for different reasons. She had noticed that the other members of the team had been giving her the cold shoulder lately when she asked for help. She did not understand why. She was the new person on the team and needed a great deal of help. She was having trouble keeping up with the others on the team, and she was nervous that Steve G. might notice. Almost involuntarily, Molly spoke up: "This will be fun; we can spend more time together and show everyone what a great group we are."

Questions:

1. Did Steve G. lack empathy toward those who report to him? What other emotionally intelligent leadership capacities might he lack?
2. Should Steve G. have used a different approach with his manager Paul instead of appeasement?
3. What should the members of team Alpha Dog do? Should they attempt to talk to Steve G. about this or just ignore the situation?
4. Are the increased work hours a realistic option? If the solution of increased work hours is imposed, what will eventually happen?

Student Quotes

I personally learn the unwritten rules of the internal workings of an organization by observation. Observing how people within the organization communicate with one another is a great way to learn how to communicate with other employees. However, there is a downside to this approach. If you read too much into an employee who isn't viewed as an appropriate example of how people should conduct themselves, then you learn those negative behaviors.

To be honest, the best way [to understand how to work in a group] is to enter a position and learn through mistakes. This can be accomplished if you provide an acclimation period wherein outgoing . . . and incoming executives work as a pair for a substantial period of time to truly understand the internal workings of the organization.

Someone learns the rules and workings through a strong leader and role model. A leader's job is to make sure that everyone involved is well informed of rules and regulations. It is a responsibility to teach and not assume that people will read the handbook. A leader can lead and teach through example.

When I'm first joining an organization, I limit my active participation. Instead, I spend my time watching the body language of long-time members. I notice (1) their manner of interaction with each other and (2) their reaction to other newcomers in the group. From these interactions, I infer social norms.

ADDITIONAL RESOURCES

Denning, S. (2004). *Squirrel, Inc.: A fable of leadership through storytelling.* San Francisco: Jossey-Bass.

Hesselbein, F., Goldsmith, M., & Beckhard, R. (Eds.). (1997). *The organization of the future.* San Francisco: Jossey-Bass.

4

Consciousness of Self

✦ Focus

Consciousness of self is obviously all about your identity,
your priorities, your values, your strengths, your goals, and
so on. As Helgeson (2001) found in her research, people need
to clearly understand themselves and what they have to offer
to determine the best way for them to contribute and make a
difference. If you are not working to better understand your
motives, values, and inner workings, who will? Not only will
this introspection result in some answers, but the *process* itself
is also critical. When was the last time you had fun? Who
were you with? What were you doing? Did you feel motivated?
Having an awareness of these and other factors can help you
create *more* happiness. The more you know about the values,
activities, people, organizations, topics, and environments that
energize you, the better equipped you are to place yourself in
situations that will bring out your best.

✦ Learning Objectives

- To practice self-reflective thinking and writing
- To explore skills and emotions related to completing a task
- To identify personal strengths that contribute to completing a task successfully

Consciousness of Self
Module 5, Activity 1: Getting It Done

By Marcy Levy Shankman & Scott J. Allen

Think about a time recently when you were successful at accomplishing something that was important to you (for example, doing well in a class or accomplishing a task). Describe that accomplishment here:

What did you do well to experience this success? Be specific. How did you feel . . .

- Before the experience?

- During the experience?

- After the experience?

What do you want to remember from this experience?

(Continued)

What strengths do you want to draw from in the future?

1. _____

2. _____

3. _____

Consciousness of Self
Module 5, Activity 2: Personal Action Plan

By Marcy Levy Shankman & Scott J. Allen

As you think about yourself in relation to emotionally intelligent leadership, consider the following questions:

What aspect(s) of emotionally intelligent leadership would you like to know more about? (Refer to the list of capacities offered in the Introduction or Appendix A for more information.)

Who can help you learn more?

Which specific capacity is a strength that you want to work on more?

What will be your first step in doing this?

(Continued)

How will you know that you've improved? What are your measures of success?

Which EIL capacity, if mastered, will take your leadership abilities to the next level?

What will be your first step in doing this?

How will you know that you've improved? What are your measures of success?

✦ Student Quotes

It is crucial to know your strengths, feelings, etc. By knowing and being in touch with these you can more effectively control them and put them to use.

If a leader is unaware of how their actions affect others, then they can have no way of gauging how these actions can change the dynamic of the group as a whole.

A person must closely monitor their own behavior around others and their reactions, both external and internal, in different circumstances.

Reflect on your behavior. After reflection, one should follow with evaluation. How did I react to situation "X," and was it appropriate? How would I act differently in the future when faced with a similar situation?

It's important to evaluate your actions to see if they are having a beneficial impact. I usually edit my actions and responses in my mind before actually doing them. But sometimes my emotions get the best of me and I just blurt things out.

ADDITIONAL RESOURCES

Books

Avolio, B., & Luthans, F. (2006). *The high impact leader*. New York: McGraw Hill.

Covey, S. R. (2004). *The seven habits of highly effective people: Powerful lessons in personal change*. New York: Fireside.

Goleman, D. (1998). *Working with emotional intelligence*. New York: Bantam Books.

Helgeson, S. (2001). *Thriving in 24/7: Six strategies for taming the new world of work*. New York: The Free Press.

Higher Education Research Institute. (1996). *A social change model of leadership development: Guidebook version III*. Los Angeles: University of California Los Angeles Higher Education Research Institute.

Rost, J. (1993). *Leadership for the 21st century*. Westport, CT: Praeger.

Segal, J. (1997). *Raising your emotional intelligence: A practical guide*. New York: Henry Holt.

Movies

Avatar (2009)

Dead Poets Society (1989)

5

Emotional Self-Perception

✦ Focus

In essence, emotional self-perception is about identifying your emotions and reactions and their impact on you. Emotional self-perception means that individuals are acutely aware of their feelings (in real time). In addition, emotional self-perception means understanding how these feelings lead to behaviors. Having emotional self-perception also means that emotionally intelligent leaders have a choice as to how they respond. This capacity enables one to differentiate between the emotions felt and the actions taken. In most situations, both healthy and unhealthy responses are available.

✦ Learning Objectives

- To develop greater emotional literacy to enhance effectiveness and awareness
- To learn strategies for enhancing emotional self-perception
- To identify and experience the connections among behaviors, activities, and emotional reactions

Emotional Self-Perception
Module 6, Activity 1: Name Your Emotions

By Wes Schaub

Write as many emotions as you can under the two headings; place the emotions closest to love and fear at the top and work to the bottom. Circle those that you experience on a daily basis.

Love	Fear
_____	_____
_____	_____
_____	_____
_____	_____
_____	_____
_____	_____
_____	_____
_____	_____
_____	_____
_____	_____
_____	_____
_____	_____

Emotional Self-Perception
Module 6, Activity 2: Emotional Log

By Wes Schaub

Based on the list created in the previous activity, keep a journal of your feelings over the next two days. Be specific in naming the emotion. Avoid broad emotional categories like happy or sad; be as specific as possible, like *elated* or *despondent*. Make sure you include both positive and negative emotions.

Date/Time _____ Emotion _____

Associated Behavior _____

Date/Time _____ Emotion _____

Associated Behavior _____

Date/Time _____ Emotion _____

Associated Behavior _____

Date/Time _____ Emotion _____

Associated Behavior _____

Date/Time _____ Emotion _____

Associated Behavior _____

Date/Time _____ Emotion _____

Associated Behavior _____

Date/Time _____ Emotion _____

Associated Behavior _____

Emotional Self-Perception
Module 6, Activity 3: Stronger Emotions

By Wes Schaub

To better understand the range of emotions we experience and what triggers them, watch a few episodes of your favorite television show or your favorite movie and respond to the following questions after each viewing. Note differences and similarities among the experiences.

I watched (TV show or movie)

_____

Date/Time _____ Emotion _____

The scene that affected me most was _____

What triggered the emotion?

Did the character experience something I face on a consistent basis?

How did the character's actions impact others around him or her?

How do others respond to me when I am in a similar state?

What is the emotion trying to tell me?

I watched (TV show or movie)

_____

Date/Time _____ Emotion _____

The scene that affected me most was _____

What triggered the emotion?

Did the character experience something I face on a consistent basis?

How did the character's actions impact others around him or her?

How do others respond to me when I am in a similar state?

What is the emotion trying to tell me?

Emotional Self-Perception
Module 6, Activity 4: Daydream Diary

By Wes Schaub

Learning to release negative feelings in an effective way is a helpful skill. One way to better manage the whole range of your emotions is to track your daydreams. When your mind wanders, hold those thoughts and write them down here. This process can help you track how your subconscious thoughts affect your moods and responses.

Daydream Situation: _____

Why are you thinking about the daydream?

What emotions or feelings do you associate with the daydream?

What is the best way for you to attend to this emotion?

If the daydream relates to a problem, what is the ideal solution?

How do you get there?

Daydream Situation: _____

Why are you thinking about the daydream?

What emotions or feelings do you associate with the daydream?

What is the best way for you to attend to this emotion?

If the daydream relates to a problem, what is the ideal solution?

How do you get there?

✦ A Case Study: Looking In, Looking Out

MBA Student

During her sophomore year, Paula decided to go through formal sorority recruitment, and she ended up accepting a bid to join Omega Rho Sigma (ORS). As a new member of ORS, she never envisioned herself in a leadership position in the chapter; however, over the course of her time in the sorority, she was honored to hold two different executive board offices.

First she was selected by the members of the executive board to become treasurer after the slated treasurer had resigned. She immediately stepped into this position ready to dedicate everything she had to it. She looked at the chapter budget numerous times, read through all of the manuals provided by the national organization, and prepared spreadsheets to track everyone's dues for the upcoming fall semester. She struggled to "hit the ground running," however, because of mistakes that Penny, the previous treasurer, had made. Penny, who had resigned as treasurer immediately before Paula stepped in, had kept incomplete records. Paula had a difficult time discerning who owed dues from the previous semester and what bills had been left unpaid. Worst of all, the budget Penny had created did not come close to adding up correctly, so Paula had to redo the budget halfway into the year.

Paula felt a bit overwhelmed—she was brand new in her role and trying to fix all of the chapter's financial problems. Unfortunately, she lost a lot of respect for the former treasurer and did not take the time to try to understand what she might have been going through that would have caused her to resign her position. Paula was so wrapped up in balancing the chapter checking account that she didn't take the time to talk directly with Penny. As such, Paula lost out on the opportunity to get a better understanding of the chapter's financial situation.

At the end of her term, Paula was slated as chapter president. Slating was a process that her sorority used to select their executive boards for the coming year. Instead of running campaigns for different positions, members of the chapter split up by class level, decide on the woman who would be best for each position, and give their results to what is called a slating committee. The slating committee then looks at the results from each of the four classes and compiles a list of the positions, with a woman's name next to each, for the chapter to vote on.

Paula was shocked to learn that her sisters saw her as the person best suited to serve as president. She felt many different emotions, but most of all, she felt the pressure of being president. She didn't want to let the women in the chapter down. Ironically, her biggest struggle was working with the new treasurer.

Betsy, the new treasurer, was a little disorganized but appeared ready to work. Paula thought she was doing a good job until the emails started pouring in at the end of the semester. The subject lines read "Check never deposited" or "Need to find out how much money I still owe." These were clearly questions to be answered by Betsy, but obviously this wasn't happening.

Paula right away let her advisor know that members were having problems with Betsy. They decided to sit down with Betsy to let her know what had been brought to their attention. Betsy shared that she had been having some serious health problems but that she would try to do a better job at completing her duties.

The next semester came and unfortunately the problem grew worse. Eventually, Betsy stopped answering emails, and she quit keeping records of transactions. Paula and the chapter advisor sat down with Betsy again to discuss what was happening. Betsy confided that her health problems had grown worse but that she still really wanted to keep her position as a way to take her mind off the other issues going on in her life. She finished the year as treasurer, but the chapter was again left in a poor financial state.

Questions:

1. When Paula took over for Penny, how did she seem to feel? What emotions might have kept her from working with Penny directly?
2. Why was Paula surprised to be slated as president?
3. What range of emotions might Paula have been experiencing? What were they based on?
4. How else could Paula have handled the situation with Betsy when the problems were first discovered?
5. How could Betsy have better managed the situation? What emotions might have motivated her to keep her position? What was holding her back from being successful?

← Student Quotes

To identify your own emotions, reactions, and possibly their impact, you have to first know yourself. As silly and obvious as that might sound, it is essential in making these identifications. Why do I do things the way I do? Why does this upset me but that doesn't? Why did I do it this way and not that way? What are my motivations? Why do I feel this way? Do I have a reason to feel this way? Where am I going at this point in my life? How did that event (or person) at X time affect my life and make me who I am today?

Someone demonstrates emotional self-perception by accepting himself as an emotional being and allowing himself to express his emotions to others.

Self-perception is about self-evaluation and taking note of how I react to certain environments and situations, how the outcomes affect me, and how I can make those situations better.

I think a big part of recognizing emotions comes from how you identify with those around you. The more in tune you are with your surroundings, the more in tune you are with yourself.

I shoulder many emotions, constantly maintaining an optimal level of stability. Image goes a long way when you are at the forefront of an organization. I identify what emotions I am feeling: frustration, stress, anger, disappointment, excitement, pride; accordingly, I deal with them internally and in private so I can constantly portray an image of stability to others.

You identify your emotional self-perception in part by comparison to others. We look at ourselves in comparison to what others do, what they think about us, and how they respond to us. Even though this is something within yourself, I think that we as humans are always looking to others.

ADDITIONAL RESOURCES

Harper, C. (2008). *Building the best you: A two-year discovery journal.* New York: Sterling.

Harrell, K. (2005). *Attitude is everything: 10 life-changing steps to turning attitude into action*. New York: HarperBusiness.

His Holiness the Dalai Lama. (2007). *How to see yourself as you really are*. New York: Atria.

Orloff, J. (2009). *Emotional freedom: Liberate yourself from negative emotions and transform your life*. New York: Harmony.

6

Honest Self-Understanding

Honest self-understanding is about being aware of your own strengths and limitations. Honest self-understanding means celebrating and honoring your strengths and talents while acknowledging and addressing your limitations. Honest self-understanding means accepting the good and bad about your personality, abilities, and ideas. When emotionally intelligent leaders demonstrate honest self-understanding, they embody a foundational capacity of effective leadership—the ability to see a more holistic self and understand how this impacts their leadership.

❧ Learning Objectives

- To express personal observations on identity, image, strengths, challenges, hopes, and fears
- To demonstrate positive "self-talk"—the opportunity to present yourself in a positive light through public speaking
- To practice self-disclosure skills and how to give and receive feedback

Honest Self-Understanding
Module 8, Activity 1: Looking Inward

By Amy Kautz

Step 1. Draw an outline of a person's head and shoulders.
   Fill in the outline with your personal thoughts about your strengths, challenges, hopes, and fears.

Step 2. Find someone whose feedback is important to you and share your drawing with this person. After you've shared your personal thoughts, ask them whether they agree and what else they might add.

Honest Self-Understanding
Module 9, Activity 2: The Mirror and Its Reflection

By Lucy Croft

Take a few minutes to respond to the following questions:

What makes me happy?

What challenges me?

What are my core values?

What do I stand for?

What motivates me?

When do I feel I most alive?

Find two people to share these thoughts with and get their reactions to your ideas.

Person 1: _____

Person 2: _____

← Student Quotes

If leaders are unsure of themselves, they cannot help others because they may second-guess themselves or change their minds often.

When a leader doesn't understand herself, it makes it extremely difficult for that leader to set consistent boundaries and have consistent practices. This leads to uneven enforcement of rules, which can greatly affect others.

If leaders can't understand themselves, how can they understand others? When others feel they are not understood, they respond with frustration or uninvolvement.

Ideally a leader is aware of his or her own strengths and weaknesses. This self-understanding can then be shared with the group they are trying to lead so that they understand how the leader operates. Possibly more important, though, is how an individual's high self-understanding encourages others to pursue an understanding of themselves as well.

When a leader understands herself, she can identify her biases and try to eliminate them from interactions with teammates.

If a leader is unsure about how he is acting, it affects others. He then has no way of gauging how these actions can change the dynamic of the group as a whole.

ADDITIONAL RESOURCES

Buckingham, M., & Clifton, D. O. (2001). *Now, discover your strengths.* New York: Free Press.

Covey, S. R. (2004). *The seven habits of highly effective people: Powerful lessons in personal change.* New York: Fireside.

Cramer, K. D., & Wasiak, J. (2008). *Change the way you see yourself through asset-based thinking.* Philadelphia, PA: Running Press.

Maxwell, J. C. (2007). *Talent is never enough: Discover the choices that will take you beyond your talent.* Nashville, TN: Thomas Nelson.

7

Healthy Self-Esteem

➤✦

✦ Focus

Having a balanced sense of self is the basis for healthy self-esteem. Emotionally intelligent leaders possess a high level of self-worth, are confident in their abilities, and are willing to stand up for what they believe in. They are also balanced by a sense of humility and the ability to create space for the opinions, perspectives, and thoughts of others. Singh (2006) found that psychologists identify high self-esteem as "the most important trait" of a person who is happy, healthy, and successful (p. 81). Healthy self-esteem therefore means recognizing your own self-worth, believing in your abilities, knowing yourself well enough to stand up for what you believe in, and being strong when you feel challenged. The "healthy" part means that you hold yourself in check—that you have some humility. You accept yourself, your strengths and your limitations, without arrogance or self-deprecation. This humility helps you have a balanced sense of self.

✦ Learning Objectives

- To reflect on self-perceptions as they relate to self-esteem
- To acknowledge the perceptions of others and how that relates to healthy self-esteem
- To explore how the environment influences our ability to understand the context in which we work with others

Healthy Self-Esteem
Module 10, Activity 1: Self-Guided Tour

Circle the answer that best describes you. There are no right or wrong answers.

Caution: You may find you are responding to the questions in terms of how you would ideally like to be. Resist that temptation and answer, instead, from a place of complete self-honesty.

1. When you make a mistake do you tend to . . .
    a. Feel ashamed and embarrassed?
    b. Say, "Who me? I never make mistakes." But if I did make one, I would immediately correct it and hope no one was watching.
    c. Have no fear owning up to it in public and open to receiving help from others in fixing it?
2. On average, when you look at yourself in the mirror what do you believe you see?
    a. Someone who is attractive and confident.
    b. Someone who is average and often unsure about what to do in life.
    c. Someone who is ugly and insecure.
3. When you are dealing with a problem in your life, what do you tend to do?
    a. Blame everyone or anything that I think caused the situation. It's rarely my fault.
    b. Complain and vent to anyone willing to listen but rarely address my personal responsibility for the issue.
    c. Take responsibility for my thoughts, words, and actions because if I take ownership, I am not a victim to the situation.
4. If my wants and needs are different from those of others I am likely to . . .
    a. Give up and give in. I'd accommodate.
    b. Say, "My way or the highway!" I argue until I get my way.
    c. Try to avoid them altogether. Why bother trying to get my needs on the table? Mine aren't important, and neither are theirs.
    d. Create a win/win solution.

(Continued)

5. When you think about the greater purpose of your life what do you tend to think?
   a. I feel like I am drifting. I am ashamed to admit it, but I don't know what I should be doing or even where to start.
   b. I have a general picture of what I want to do and what I am capable of creating for my life.
   c. I am on course with my purpose, and know I am capable of creating whatever my heart desires for my life.

6. When I make a commitment to myself I often tend to . . .
   a. Break it before the end of the hour. I am terrible at following up on my self-goals.
   b. Do it with hesitation and fear because I so desperately hate disappointment.
   c. Stick to it with conviction and await the rewards that I believe will come from it.

7. When you talk to yourself (you know, that little voice in your head) what does it tend to sound like?
   a. Critical and negative. I often put myself down and beat myself up emotionally.
   b. Fairly confident and supportive, but I still have those days when my self-talk holds back my true greatness.
   c. Extremely confident and helpful. I have learned to become my own best friend and weed out my limiting thoughts from the empowering ones.

8. How do you often react to what other people say about you?
   a. I take things personally, and if I think someone is saying something negative about me I take it too much to heart.
   b. I get defensive and often respond with an equal, if not greater, negative reaction to them.
   c. I value what others have to say about me—but honestly—I know who I am, and other peoples' opinions have no bearing on my self-worth.

(Adapted from and reproduced with approval from the National Association of Self-Esteem.)

Healthy Self-Enhancers

The following thoughts correspond to the questions in the Self-Guided Tour.

1. It is quite "normal," and human, to not enjoy making mistakes! That is why we often feel embarrassed, deny their existence, and/or blame others for our errors. We believe that the best way is to admit your mistakes, learn from them, and take corrective action. After all, a mistake is a mistake—no more, no less.

2. We live in a society that emphasizes glamour and sex appeal. That is why most of us strive to achieve external beauty, but oftentimes we lose our uniqueness in the process. If we can accept the things we'd like to change without badmouthing or beating up on ourselves, we've come a long way toward self-acceptance.

3. Taking responsibility for your own thoughts, words, and actions is more easily said than done. However, we believe the quality of your well-being is directly proportional to how much self-responsibility you are willing to take. When we blame others or outside events for our position or condition in life we lock ourselves into a prison of pain. There truly is freedom in taking ownership for how we respond to what happens to us in life.

4. Your wants, needs, and self-worth are as important as those of anyone else. However, that doesn't mean others will automatically respect them. If you silence your own voice, others will not know what you want or need. It's up to you to claim your needs as important and learn how to respectfully assert yourself. With practice, you'll be amazed at how this will become second nature.

5. Have you ever wondered "Why am I here?" or "What am I supposed to do in life?" If so, you're in very good company. This is one of the most fundamental life decisions you can make. Your purpose is about what you plan to achieve and the kind of person you want to be. Your character and your habits will lead you to be healthier, happier, and more successful. What are you good at? What do you really enjoy? These are two good places to

(Continued)

look when you're trying to decide your direction. Your life has the potential to be so much more than you might imagine. The most important thing is that your life has meaning for you.

6. If you've ever heard the phrase "your word is your bond," you'll understand why honoring commitments is an aspect of healthy self-esteem. A commitment is a pledge, and a pledge is a guarantee. When you make a commitment to yourself or others you're putting your integrity on the line. As you learn to demonstrate that you can be counted on to do what you say, you build your self-esteem and your credibility at the same time. That way you and others will know that "you walk your talk."

7. If you're like most people you say things to yourself you wouldn't tolerate coming from another person. Negative self-talk scares us out of taking positive risks so we can avoid failure. Here's how you can start to build positive, self-empowering inner dialogues. First, recognize your negative self-talk. Next, interrupt the pattern; tell yourself "Erase that. Here's what I really mean!" The last step is to give yourself a positive instruction, like "I can do this. I'm up to the task," or "Let's try it on for size." The more you replace your negative self-talk with positive self-talk, the more your self-esteem and self-confidence will grow.

8. When you put more weight on your own judgment than on others,' it's easier to keep their words in perspective without becoming defensive. Your strong sense of self-worth allows you to maintain your power and still hear what others have to say without feeling bad about yourself.

The finest things in life are neither costly nor hard to find. They are waiting right within you.
—Japanese proverb

Reference

National Association of Self-Esteem, http://www.self-esteem-nase.org/rate.php. (Reproduced with approval from the National Association of Self-Esteem.)

Healthy Self-Esteem
Module 10, Activity 2: Others' Perceptions of You

By Sabrina Ryan

List at least ten adjectives and/or nouns that you would use to describe yourself right now.

Now think about how others perceive you.

List people who know you well; consider family, friends, coworkers, peers, and so on	How does he or she perceive you?	How does your perception differ from the person you identified?

Healthy Self-Esteem
Module 10, Activity 3: Striking Resemblance

By Sabrina Ryan

Responding to the following statements will help you think more deeply about yourself. Using the animal descriptions on the next page, complete the sentence, then write why you chose that description.

- When I find that tasks aren't getting done in the time I would like to see them done, I behave most like:

- I am the "most successful" as:

- When I am angry, I act like:

- When things are sailing along nicely, I behave most like:

- When I disagree with my friends, I behave most like:

- When I am in charge of a project, I behave most like:

- When I am working in a team environment, I behave most like:

- When I work alone, I behave most like:

- When I am happy, I am:

- When I disagree with the direction in which an organization is heading, I behave like:

- When I feel at my worst, I behave like:

- When I see a goal clearly and am inspired to head toward it, I behave most like:

Animal Descriptions

Monkey: Fun-loving, full of jokes most of the time, loves to make people laugh, rarely serious

Donkey: Strong-willed, hard-headed, rarely jokes, may be a jerk at times, may not have a reason for behaving like this

Ostrich: Shy and quiet, rarely speaks in a large group, does a lot of internal processing

Lion: Loud, strong-willed, takes charge, speaks out

Healthy Self-Esteem
Module 10, Activity 4: Reflection

By Sabrina Ryan

Consciousness of Self

1. How would you describe your self-esteem?

2. What's healthy about your self-esteem?

3. What are your opportunities for improvement?

Consciousness of Others

1. How does your self-esteem influence your relationships?

2. What's healthy about your self-esteem in relation to others?

3. What are your opportunities for improvement?

Consciousness of Context

1. How does your environment influence your self-esteem?

2. How does your environment promote a healthy level of self-esteem?

3. How does your environment interfere with developing a healthy level of self-esteem?

✦ Case Study: A Young Leader Is Elected to the Students' Union

Veronika Julia Korner

Students' Union (SU) is a student organization at many universities in Hungary dedicated to student governance. SUs are run by students for students, and for the most part they are independent of the institution. The purpose of these organizations is to represent students internally and externally on local and national issues. The SU usually has its own building or its own office on campus. The SU also assumes responsibility for providing a variety of services for the students. Students can get involved in its management through participation in committees, councils, and general meetings, or by becoming an elected officer. Many SUs are highly politicized associations; interestingly, they often serve as a training ground for aspiring politicians.

Janie is a freshman who was elected to the SU in the fall semester. Although enthusiastic about the position, she has no idea what to do or whom to work with. The only people she knows are her classmates and the people who encouraged her to seek election.

The SU has five boards: financial, social services, student affairs, academic affairs, and recreation and sports. Each board has its elected chairman for the semester. Suzie, a third-year student and literature major, is the chairman for the financial board.

Janie gets assigned to work with Suzie. Suzie has difficulty finding her own voice as a leader; however, she is good at interpreting situations and the power networks within the SU and the university. Suzie is hard-working and achievement-oriented. After a couple of months she gains people's trust and begins to build up her own network within the institution.

As the school year passes, Suzie becomes more and more confident in her position as chairman of the financial board. Janie becomes close with Suzie, and they develop a strong working relationship. Suzie decides she wants to run for the presidency and asks Janie to help her do it. They run a successful campaign and she gets elected. The campaign, however, is harsh and hard-fought. Suzie struggles with expressing herself throughout the campaign, but her network is strong and supports her through her inability to moderate her reactions at times. She truly struggles with maintaining her self-esteem. Throughout the campaign, Suzie confides in Janie about personal problems (a breakup with her boyfriend and her bad GPA). Suzie also has a difficult time handling the stress and conflict.

Janie thinks Suzie isn't ready to be president—that her election was premature. In Hungary, academia is still male-dominated, and it is unusual for a female with limited leadership experience to be elected. For Suzie it is difficult to work through the personal attacks made during the campaign. She is not sure who she can trust, and she is insecure in her new position. Janie begins to doubt whether Suzie truly wants the position.

Janie talks with Suzie a lot and wants to help her. To Suzie's detriment, she frequently panics because she is unsure of whether she can effectively handle the stress and the responsibility.

Questions:
  1. Would you describe Suzie's self-esteem as healthy? If so, why? If not, why not?
  2. How does self-esteem influence the work of a leader? How does it influence those around her?
  3. What could Suzie do to enhance her self-esteem? What can Janie do to help Suzie?
  4. How will the group be affected over the long term if this issue is not resolved?

Healthy self-esteem is not arrogance. It is an ability to interact with others in a positive and rational manner that exudes some form of personal acceptance. You are comfortable with yourself enough to manage daily experiences that may question your ability or challenge your sense of who you are.

Usually when I'm under stress, with homework coming up or when I'm taking a test, I have to choose to feel relaxed and optimistic and not doomed . . . I think college students are learning to control emotions in every challenge they face, and are probably learning more from mistakes they make. Those who have faced adversity before college will be better prepared for challenges in college.

Healthy self-esteem is primarily about knowing who you are deep down inside. It's about knowing the person you are when no one is watching. Healthy self-esteem involves knowing your background, biases, prejudices, communication style, and emotions. To have healthy self-esteem, one needs to be in tune with every part of their being.

A healthy self-esteem is knowing what you are good at and knowing what you need to work on.

If you trust yourself to make choices, whether difficult or easy, you will build inner strength that comes out in your work and encourages others. Believing in yourself is a great way to develop a healthy self-esteem, but one should never allow that to develop into arrogance.

Healthy self-esteem can be seen across a room. First, the person has good posture and a pleasant manner. When I talk to the person, she replies without qualifications and with no apologies for her opinions. But the person is not arrogant. She carefully considers her thoughts and is willing to change her opinions when good evidence is presented. Her self-worth is not tied to being correct all the time.

ADDITIONAL RESOURCES

Books

Basco, M. R. (2000). *Never good enough: How to use perfectionism to your advantage without letting it ruin your life.* New York: Free Press.

Harrell, K. (2005). *Attitude is everything: 10 life-changing steps to turning attitude into action.* New York: HarperBusiness.

Kanter, R. M. (2004). *Confidence: How winning streaks and losing streaks begin and end.* New York: Crown Business.

McKay, M., & Fanning, P. (2000). *Self-esteem: A proven program of cognitive techniques for assessing, improving, and maintaining your self-esteem* (3rd ed.). New York: MJF Books.

Patterson, R. J. (2000). *The assertiveness workbook: How to express your ideas and stand up for yourself at work and in relationships.* New York: MJF Books.

Singh, D. (2006). *Emotional intelligence at work: A professional guide* (3rd ed.). New Delhi, India: Response Books.

Online Video Clips

Dove Self-Esteem Fund (http://www.youtube.com/watch?v=7rSjh52fGTg)

Body Image and Self-Esteem (www.youtube.com/watch?v=gC9g-1MJdE4 &feature=related)

8

Emotional Self-Control

✦ Focus

Emotional self-control entails consciously moderating both our emotions and our reactions. Although feeling emotions and being aware of them is part of this, so too is regulating them. Emotional self-control is about both awareness (being conscious of feelings) and action (managing emotions and knowing when and how to show them). Recognizing feelings, understanding how and when to demonstrate those feelings appropriately, and taking responsibility for our emotions (versus being victims of them) are critical components of this capacity.

✦ Learning Objectives

- To enhance your understanding of the components of emotional self-control
- To explore the implications of not demonstrating emotional self-control
- To identify personal "hot buttons" or triggers for strong, negative emotions

Emotional Self-Control
Module 11, Activity 1: Emotional Worst-Case Scenario

By Amy Kautz

Describe in detail a recent situation (within the last few weeks if possible) in which you lost your temper (an example of an "emotional worst-case scenario").

1. What was it about?

2. Where did it happen?

3. Who did it involve?

4. Who witnessed it?

5. When did it happen?

6. What did you say?

7. What were the reactions of others?

8. What else of importance do you recall?

9. How did you feel during the scenario?
   What were your physical reactions, (e.g., sweating, teeth clenching, upset stomach)?

   What thoughts (such as "seeing red," extreme emotions, nothing) were going through your head during the scenario?

(Continued)

10. How did you feel after the scenario was over? Physical reactions?

Thoughts?

11. Looking back, can you see a trigger or hot button that may have led to this "Emotional Worst-Case Scenario"?

12. Identify ways you can act or react differently in the future. Look at your physical and emotional triggers. How can you stop, change, or reframe your reaction to the situation?

Two important aspects of emotional self-control are recognizing how stress affects us and being aware of our hot buttons.
—Shankman and Allen (2008, p. 43)

❧ Case Study: The Green Streak Weekly

Mike Spinelli

The *Green Streak Weekly* is a primary news source at Centennial University. It is a student-run newspaper with a strong reputation on campus. For years, the *Green Streak Weekly* has been recognized nationally for its commitment to excellence in journalism and page layouts.

The newspaper is made possible only through the dedication of students who volunteer their time and energy. Being an editor for the paper involves a large time commitment and good time management so that deadlines are met. The formal structure consists of an editor-in-chief, a managing editor, numerous section editors, and writers and copy editors. The editor-in-chief serves as the ultimate authority for the paper. This person has the final say on what goes to print and ultimately is responsible for content.

Mary is a newly appointed features editor. She is an underclasswoman and likes to stay busy. She is in charge of a well-known campus service organization and is an active member of campus ministry; she even sings in the campus choir. She tends to overextend herself at times but is more than willing to put forth the effort to fulfill her responsibilities.

Sarah is also in a newly appointed position. After four years of working her way up through the ranks of the newspaper, she has just been elected the editor-in-chief. Many on staff felt that she would make a good editor-in-chief because of her accomplishments as a section editor. She is a good writer and layout designer, and she pays exceptional attention to detail.

It is the week before finals, and the last issue of the year is due to come out. Because of election timing, this is only the second issue under the new newspaper administration. Because it is also the end of the semester and the last week of classes, work is piling up for the new section editors.

Mary's first feature section was a success. It was a unique concept, accompanied by a great article, interviews, and layout. Mary completed the section a day prior to her Sunday night deadline. The stage was set for Mary to be a successful features editor.

Her second and most recent issue, however, did not go so smoothly. She, like most students, got caught up in the academic work that tends to get piled on at the end of a semester. Mary had fallen behind on her homework and was having trouble completing the feature section. Desperate for help, Mary turned to her friend and co-editor Sam to help complete the section. Sam said he would help Mary by completing the interviews and by taking the pictures to accompany the interviews. Sam also offered to help Mary with the page layout—a time-consuming process.

Mary felt extremely relieved and grateful for Sam's willingness to help. Mary informed Sarah of her busy schedule and told Sarah that Sam would be doing much of the work for the coming issue. Sarah said she had no problem with this, as long as everything got done.

On the Friday before the deadline, Mary wrote the article because she knew that she had a busy weekend ahead of her. She had three papers to write for classes (all of which were due early in the coming week) and an all-day campus ministry retreat on Sunday. She was also singing with the campus choir in the halftime show at a National Basketball Association (NBA) game the following Tuesday night, for which they had been practicing all semester. Sam was responsible for having everything on the page by Sunday night so that the section could go through the first round of editing before final layout on Tuesday night.

Mary left for the basketball game Tuesday evening expecting to come back and have everything finished with the feature section. To her dismay, Sam had not begun to lay out the page, nor had he completed all of the necessary interviews. To make matters worse, Sam was nowhere to be found and not answering his phone or responding to texts.

When Mary walked into the newsroom, Sarah greeted her with an angry, disappointed outburst. Sarah reminded Mary that she had volunteered for her position and that part of her responsibility was to ensure that everything was completed in a timely manner. Sarah also informed Mary that she had missed her section's deadline because her pages were not completed on Sunday night.

Mary was disappointed and angry at herself. She was disappointed in herself for not following through on her commitment. She was also angry at Sam for his failure to follow through on his promise. She tried to explain to Sarah all the pressure that she was under and that she had taken every possible measure to ensure that the pages would be completed on time. She tried to remain composed but ended up in tears. Instead of trying to remedy the situation, Sarah responded hastily. She told Mary that she needed to set a tone early in her administration, so she was going to take the pages away from Mary's section and fill the blank pages with advertisements instead. And she suggested that if this happened again, Mary would be replaced by someone else who could manage the responsibility.

Questions:
1. How would you describe the ways in which emotions were managed in this situation?
2. How might Sarah's response have been different if she had been empathetic to Mary's situation?
3. How important is it for a leader to manage his or her emotions?
4. How might Mary have handled the situation differently?

← Student Quotes

Emotional self-control may be hard for students, because they are emotional and still growing . . .

I've had to moderate my emotions in front of other members of an organization who were not paying attention, and not following directions. I had to keep myself calm to describe what they were doing wrong, which can be difficult because we are often under time constraints.

I believe that all college students must moderate their emotions, especially if they are also involved in groups and activities outside of their classes. These other groups cause more emotional stress than a normal class schedule, so oftentimes the saying "leave your baggage at the door" comes into play and one must manage emotions to succeed.

I once led a group with an executive member who was the polar opposite of my passive and understanding nature—this person exuded arrogance and a persona of "I am right, and even if I am not, I am going to tell you I am right and continue to argue with you." As president, I am sure my frustrations were sometimes evident, but "frustration" was probably scratching the surface of my dislike for these compromising situations and the difficulty this person presented. However, self-control and continuously trying to balance this individual with my desires were best for the group. I don't think this "moderation" is exuded by many students because they have probably never operated in the environment of collegiate student organizations before. The sense of freedom presented in college makes comparing previous (high school) leadership different because those past experiences were most likely heavily monitored by teachers or parents.

There are times when people in my organization would anger me. Instead of taking my frustration out on others, I take some time to get over it. When I'm ready, I have to talk it out, otherwise it won't go away. Self-control is hard, but just keep in mind the consequences of no self-control.

ADDITIONAL RESOURCES

Books

Carlson, R. (2000). *Don't sweat the small stuff for teens: Simple ways to keep your cool in stressful times.* New York: Hyperion.

Ellis, A., & Tafrate, R. C. (2000). *How to control your anger before it controls you.* New York: Citadel Press.

Helmstetter, S. (1982). *What to say when you talk to yourself.* New York: Pocket Books.

Jeffers, S. (2006). *Feel the fear . . . and do it anyway.* New York: Ballantine Books.

Shankman, M. L., & Allen, S. J. (2008). *Emotionally intelligent leadership: A guide for college students.* San Francisco: Jossey-Bass.

Films/TV

Anger Management (2003)

Billy Madison (2005)

Punk'd (any episode, any season)

The Real World (any episode, any season)

9

Authenticity

← Focus

Authenticity is about being transparent and trustworthy. It is a complex concept that emphasizes the importance of living in a way in which your words match your actions and vice versa. This is no small order. Being authentic means, in part, that emotionally intelligent leaders follow through on commitments and present themselves and their motives in an open and honest manner. This may sound simple, but it is not. You must know yourself well enough to know what you can honestly commit to and then follow through on this promise. Authenticity is also about being true to your values, feelings, and ideas. Often the hardest part about being authentic is in your actions—do you do what you say you will do? How well do your actions align with your words?

✦ Learning Objectives

- To explore the concept of authenticity as a critical capacity for leadership
- To identify antecedents, actions, and outcomes of an authentic life
- To develop a personal commitment to being authentic

Authenticity
Module 12, Activity 1: What's My Message?

By Darbi Roberts

Step One: If my life is my message, then what message am I sending?

- How do you interact with strangers?

- Do you treat everybody fairly? Give an example.

- Do you take full responsibility for your actions? How do you do this? When don't you?

- How do you follow through on what you commit to doing?

- Is there a difference in your personality or actions when you're around other people versus when you're alone?

(*Continued*)

Step Two: What messages would you rather send?

- What kinds of messages do you want people to take away from your interactions with them?

- What messages (positive and negative) do you think other people get from observing you in group activities?

Step Three: Making changes!

- What changes do you need to make so that your actual message is more aligned with the message you want to send?

- What needs to be different about how you interact with others?

- How can you improve the alignment between your ideas and actions?

Step Four: Start with small steps

What action(s) can you take in the next twenty-four hours that would exhibit one of these changes?

Authenticity
Module 12, Activity 2: Your Integrity Advantage

By Darbi Roberts

To further develop your sense of authenticity, try the following. Rate yourself on the following, from 1 (low) to 10 (high):

1. You know that little things count. ____
2. You find the clear answers where others see things less clearly. ____
3. You publicly acknowledge when you make a mistake. ____
4. You develop trusting relationships. ____
5. You keep your word. ____
6. You care about the greater good. ____
7. You're honest and modest. ____

Get a second opinion.
Record the names of five people you know whom you trust.

Ask them to give you feedback on how you rated yourself on the preceding list of items. Write down their feedback. Take time to consider their input—what answers did they give that are in synch with your own? Based on their feedback, what are your strengths and areas for improvement?

(*Continued*)

Assess your environment.

Answer the following questions by circling Yes (Y) or No (N).

1. Do you spend time with people who are honest? Y N
2. Is communication among those in your circle of friends frequent, open, and honest? Y N
3. Are you comfortable admitting you've made a mistake? Y N
4. Have you said no to someone who asked you to do something that you didn't believe in? Y N
5. Do you trust the people you spend time with? Y N
6. Are you proud to tell your family about your friends? Y N

The more "Yes" answers you've given to these questions, the more supportive your environment is. Review all items with an "N" and identify ways to turn each into a "Y." What will it take?

Reference

Gostick, A., & Telford, D. (2003). *The integrity advantage.* Layton, UT: Gibbs Smith.

✦ Case Study: Who's It Really For?

Jessica Sindelar

Chi Kappa is one of Old Psi Wash University's twenty-five national sororities. The chapter on campus is seventy years old. The focus of the organization is building relationships, helping young women make connections and philanthropic activities. Relationships are built through sisterhood events, Greek Week, date parties, and mixers; networking connections are forged through educational speakers, Founders' Day events, and visits to headquarters. Philanthropy is prioritized throughout the year through visits to soup kitchens, food banks, hospice centers, and events on campus.

One event the chapter holds annually is Disco Marathon (DM). In preparation for DM, the women of the sorority collect donations from local businesses, families, and friends. A committee helps plan activities for the evening and money raised from this event goes to a chosen philanthropy.

The problem began with the choice of the philanthropy to benefit from DM. Mallory, the philanthropy chair for Chi Kappa, was in charge of planning DM. Joyce, the previous philanthropy chair, who had started DM during her time in office, was helping Mallory plan the event. In addition, Mallory had the help of several other members of Chi Kappa Chi who volunteered to serve on the planning committee and share the workload. The committee consisted of Kelsey, Beth, Leah, Rebecca, and Jillian. Mallory and Kelsey were best friends and roommates. They considered their opinions to be more important than the opinions of the others.

The previous year, Joyce had chosen a foundation that supports breast cancer research. Numerous "disco dancers" for the event commented that they came to the event specifically because of the cause. An evaluation also showed that Joyce's decision to divide the chapter into small groups and assign those groups to various local businesses to seek out donations made a positive difference.

Mallory approached planning for DM differently. Although Joyce had shared these suggestions, Mallory did not involve the chapter as a whole by sending out the small groups to get donations. The committee later felt that many of the women were not motivated to secure donations, mostly because they had not been directly involved in the planning and fundraising. When this phase of fundraising was completed, Mallory presented to the committee the amount that had been raised, and they realized it was a considerable decrease from the previous year.

Although the lack of involvement by non–committee members was a significant factor in the decrease, the committee also felt the choice of the philanthropy had affected donations and member motivation. Joyce, Beth, Leah, Rebecca, and Jillian had suggested again choosing a philanthropy that many people could relate to or one that "tugged at the heart strings." A women's shelter and homes for children were also suggested. They even suggested sticking with last year's recipient.

Mallory and Kelsey, however, wanted to go with one of the sorority's national philanthropies: Jumpstart for a Job, an organization that helps women prepare for all aspects of a job interview. Although Joyce and the majority of the committee realized that Jumpstart for a Job was a beneficial and important organization, they felt that it didn't offer the same appeal to college students. The committee had discussed this point with Mallory tirelessly, and as the time for winter break approached, they thought she was convinced. But when classes resumed in January at the end of winter break, Mallory and Kelsey announced their decision: Jumpstart for a Job would be the recipient.

Questions:

1. How authentic were the various members of the committee, including Mallory?
2. How does a lack of authenticity affect the work of the committee? What was the impact of these actions on the outcome of Disco Marathon?
3. What could Joyce and the others have done differently to persuade Mallory?
4. If Joyce and the committee had approached Kelsey, Mallory's best friend, how might this have made a difference?

← Student Quotes

An authentic leader is someone who is consistent in her actions. An authentic leader would be the same person on the inside that she is projecting on the outside.

An authentic leader is someone who takes charge. It's a person who isn't afraid to go against the norms to make a change. This person believes in him- or herself.

An authentic leader does not try to take credit for the work of the entire group. An authentic leader will have sincere concerns for the well-being of his group members and the outcome of the group's work.

An authentic leader is willing to step back and be a follower when it is needed. They don't always need to be in charge, but when the moment arises where they need to be, they will.

An authentic leader guides people with compassion and honesty.

ADDITIONAL RESOURCES

Bronson, P. (2002). *What should I do with my life? The true story of people who answered the ultimate question.* New York: Random House.

George, B. (2007). *True north: Discover your authentic leadership.* San Francisco: Jossey-Bass.

Gostick, A., & Telford, D. (2003). *The integrity advantage.* Layton, UT: Gibbs Smith.

McKenna, P. (2006). *You can have what you want.* Carlsbad, CA: Hay House.

10

Flexibility

✦ Focus

Flexibility entails being open and adaptive to changing situations. The best laid plans don't always come to fruition, so emotionally intelligent leaders need to be responsive to change and open to feedback. By thinking creatively and using their problem-solving skills, emotionally intelligent leaders engage others in determining a new way to reach their goals. One way in which the emotionally intelligent leader demonstrates flexibility is by seeking out and using feedback from others. When others feel that their feedback is taken into consideration, they are more likely to support the final outcome or decision. Flexibility often yields better solutions. After all, each of us sees issues, problems, and challenges from a different vantage point. By working together with others and being flexible, we can achieve better solutions in terms of both outcome and process.

✦ Learning Objectives

- To learn improvisation skills to expand your ability to think creatively and handle the unexpected

- To identify examples of when you have experienced an unexpected event and how you dealt with it
- To understand that at times successful leadership depends on how well you react to unexpected circumstances
- To practice adaptive thinking as an interactive approach to influencing others

Flexibility
Module 13, Activity 1: Expert Improv Actors

By Tracy Purinton

Review the following list of characteristics of improvisational actors:

- Are present in the moment, curious, and engaged
- Listen intently
- Make specific suggestions and active choices
- Are action-oriented
- See the whole picture or scene as it is unfolding
- Meet the unexpected with a spirit of "Yes" rather than "No"
- Embrace change and seek to advance the development of the scene
- Present new ideas and leave the door open for others to do so
- Build on others' ideas and create connections and develop relationships
- Bring out the best in all other team members with the goal of making others look good (versus trying to stand out)
- Take risks
- View the unexpected as a valuable opportunity
- Are flexible, resilient, and able to play a variety of roles
- Have fun!

What if you changed the term *improvisational actors* to *good leaders*?

- Which statements in this list work? Mark with a "+"
- Which of the statements do not work? Mark with a "−"
- What additional characteristics might apply to one or both groups?

Flexibility
Module 13, Activity 2: Key Rules of Improv

By Tracy Purinton

Read through the following rules of improvisational acting:

1. The first rule—accept the offer—is never broken. All statements by improv actors are called "offers." Whatever an improv actor says—for example, "Hey, it's great to be back from the Amazon!"—the other actors must accept as reality. They can't say, "No, we're in an ice-cream store!" This is the rule that makes improv theater possible.

2. What makes improv work—what allows the group to create a satisfying, coherent story in the present moment—is the second rule, an extension of the first: the *Yes, and . . .* rule. This is the core rule of improvisational theater because it incorporates the rule of accepting the offer (*Yes!*) while requiring that an actor build on and extend what's been offered (*Yes, and . . .*).

3. The third rule is to be an active "high stakes" listener; this means to listen as if the scene's success relies on it. Be interested, not interesting!

4. The fourth rule is to adapt your role to the new reality. Don't be constrained by your own thinking about what will happen. Listen to what the other members of your team are saying and then adapt the role you are playing to fit as best you can. Be creative!

Which of these rules apply to leadership? In what ways?

Practice rule #2—write a scenario that describes a challenge you've experienced with leadership. Any time you find yourself writing "but" or any other contradicting comment, try inserting "yes, and" instead.

What happens when you apply rule #2?

What did you discover by writing your scenario using "yes, and"? How might this work for you in "real time"?

Flexibility
Module 13, Activity 3: Your Improviser/Leader Profile

By Tracy Purinton

The following roles reflect typical approaches and roles that people take in leadership opportunities. Read through this list and answer the questions below.

Captain	Do it this way!
Initiator/Conceiver	Here's the future—follow me!
Supporter/Collaborator	I'll help you do it.
Accommodator	Let's make space or room for agreement.
Coach	You can do it!
Mediator	Let's bring all the different ideas together and see where we can go.
Observer	I'm going to see how things work before I jump in.
Joiner	I'll help! Tell me what I can do!
Challenger	I'm sure there is a better way to do this.

• Which role do you tend to play most often? Which is most comfortable? This is your default approach.

• Which role is most challenging for you?

• What are the strengths of your default approach?

- How does your default approach get in the way?

- Do any of these roles tend to push your buttons?

- Which of these roles are uncomfortable or do not feel natural?

- How might you go about practicing some of these behaviors or expanding your comfort zone?

- If you talk with others, what suggestions do they have for how to expand your improvisation comfort zone?

Flexibility
Module 13, Activity 4: Mapping Your Flexibility

By Tracy Purinton

On the following line, place five "x" marks to represent times in your life when you experienced a major change.

On the left side of the line, describe the event.

On the right side of the line, describe what the experience was like. What feelings did you experience? What ideas did you have before the event and then after the event? Did you change your behavior? If so, how?

As you look at this map of major changes in your life, what patterns emerge as to how you respond to change? Consider your emotions as well as your actions. As you look at these patterns of responses, how flexible would you say you've been? In what ways?

✦ Case Study: Sink or Swim?

Andrea Kovacs

Allison is a four-year varsity member of the university swimming and diving team. As a senior, she is honored with being chosen as the team captain. As a Division II school, the university is a member of the regional athletic conference. Students at this level are recognized as student-athletes by the coaching staff, rather than athlete-students. The women's team has been a dominant force in the conference, having captured twenty-five of the past thirty conference championships. Allison's past experience as a swimmer, dedication to the team, and strong work ethic toward self-improvement have made her someone the team respects and hopes will help lead them to another championship title this season.

Allison uses an affiliative style of leadership by focusing on relationships within the team. By this point in her college career, she has developed a number of strong relationships with teammates, coaches, and university faculty and staff. She enjoys being a part of a team and working collectively toward a common goal. Prior to becoming captain, Allison took many non-positional leadership roles on the team in her actions at meets and practices. Many members turned to Allison for advice or guidance with handling school work, personal problems, or internal conflicts between teammates. Her confidence, care, and concern for the team inspired and pushed others to attain the same level of dedication to the team both in and out of the water.

Allison's level of commitment has demanded a significant amount of effort and determination. Allison becomes easily frustrated with members who do not put forth the same effort or show a high level of commitment. Although the coaching staff allows a considerable amount of flexibility in practice attendance and traveling to meets, Allison is intolerant of members who miss any team responsibility, including team functions. She believes that any absence throughout the season (which starts in September and lasts through February) should have reasonable consequences.

As the season progresses, team members begin to resent Allison because of how she treats them for missing practice. The team begins to experience conflict because of the inconsistency in leadership styles between the coach and captain. Academic responsibilities are presented as first priority by coaches, faculty, and staff. Although Allison recognizes that school is important, she knows that she's balanced her team and academic responsibilities. She figures, "If I can do it, so can they." Eventually, Allison's intolerance of her teammates' decisions causes conflict. Allison feels that the relationships she has developed and her ability to effectively motivate and guide the team are suffering.

At team meetings, Allison expresses, time and time again, the importance of training and its effect on each individual's ability to compete in pressure situations. Many members feel added pressure to perform in the face of Allison's demanding expectations. In fact, a few members become so overwhelmed with this pressure that their other commitments and responsibilities suffer. Some team members must take extended breaks from practices because they become so far behind with outside work.

Allison tries to unite the team by planning team functions outside of practices and meets. Allison polls the team frequently for ideas and suggestions about dinners, movies, and other events for team nights. Allison is open to any activity as long as everyone participates. After planning many of these events and experiencing low turnout, she tries something different to deal with the conflicts that are arising. After polling everyone, in an effort to make everyone happy Allison leaves it to the team to decide what to do. As a result, team functions now are consistently thrown together at the last minute. Plans constantly change because team members seem to point in different directions. Instead of incorporating outside fun for the team, Allison's concern for pleasing everyone has led to added frustration and team conflicts.

In this leadership position, Allison's lack of flexibility in the water (about practices and meets) combined with her overwhelming flexibility outside the water to result in a divided team.

Questions:
1. How might Allison adjust her role as captain to improve the situation for the team?
2. What outcomes resulted from Allison's inability to be flexible around practices? What outcomes resulted from her being too flexible with planning team functions?
3. How does Allison's inability to balance flexibility affect her leadership style and the team overall?
4. What steps should Allison take to improve this capacity?

Student Quotes

Flexibility is usually a plus. It allows others to be comfortable and to contribute and have a say in the process. However, being too flexible is not leadership. You have to be willing to say "no" when it comes time.

Flexibility is an asset to a leader. It allows them to appear more accommodating to others. However, too much flexibility can lead to disorganization.

Flexibility is key. Things constantly change and leaders need to react to sometimes sudden changes and make the best decisions based on the changes. The best-laid plans almost always go awry in some way. However, flexibility might be a problem in a leadership position in that too much flexibility might mean bending too much.

Flexibility equals versatility in many cases, and allows a leader to move with ease from one situation to another. However, if a leader is too flexible, it may lead to subordinates taking advantage of the leader.

Flexibility allows a leader to adapt to the individuals within a group. As we all know people are different, and to maximize a relationship, people must be treated in different ways. The biggest problem with flexibility is that when it is applied on a large scale it creates a challenge. Adapting to everyone becomes overwhelming.

I don't think organizations can operate effectively without flexibility.

ADDITIONAL RESOURCES

Brooks, R., & Goldstein, S. (2004). *The power of resilience: Achieving balance, confidence, and personal strength in your life.* New York: McGraw Hill.

Center for Creative Leadership, Gurvis, J., & Calarco, A. (2006). *Adaptability: Responding effectively to change.* Greensboro, NC: Author.

DeBono, E. (1973). *Lateral thinking: Creativity step by step.* New York: Harper Colophon.

Michalko, M. (2006). *ThinkerToys: A handbook of creative-thinking techniques* (2nd ed.). Berkeley, CA: Ten Speed Press.

Ryan, M. J. (2009). *Adaptability: How to survive change you didn't ask for.* New York: Broadway.

11

Achievement

✦ Focus

Achievement is about being driven to improve according to personal standards. An important nuance of this capacity for emotionally intelligent leadership is the role of personal standards. Individuals often know achievement when they see and feel it. Instead of letting others define what achievement looks like, emotionally intelligent leaders pursue their passions and goals to a self-determined level of accomplishment. This drive produces results and may inspire others to become more focused in their efforts or to achieve at higher levels as well. No matter what the passion is, when we are committed to demonstrating emotionally intelligent leadership, we will pursue it to a high level of achievement.

✦ Learning Objectives

- To understand the concept of achievement in relation to emotionally intelligent leadership
- To explore the influences that affect the decisions you make
- To develop an action plan for developing a specific leadership capacity

Achievement
Module 14, Activity 1: Impressions

By Sarah Spengler

In the left column, list four or five people, real or fictional, whom you admire. Leave some space between the names. These people may have had a direct or an indirect influence on you. They may or may not be famous.

In the right column, list some of their key characteristics that you admire.

People   **Characteristics**

Circle two to three characteristics that you think you can develop over the next year.

Achievement 1
Module 14, Activity 2: Action Plan

By Sarah Spengler

Complete the following sentence stems. Refer back to Activity 1, if needed.

This is my action plan for developing my leadership potential in terms of _____.

List what you will do to develop this capacity.

I will:

A mentor to help me along the way:

Next week, I will:

Next month, I will:

By the end of the year, I will:

Signature: _____

Date: _____

Achievement 2
Module 15, Activity 3: Internal and External Locus of Control

By Sarah Spengler

Consider the following ideas:

External Locus of Control
External locus of control describes a person's belief that his or her behavior is guided by fate, luck, other people, or circumstances outside of that person's control.

Internal Locus of Control
Internal locus of control describes a person's belief that his or her behavior is guided by his or her own decisions and efforts.

Identify a challenge you currently (or often) face. Choose something about which you are uncertain of the correct course of action. Describe that situation here (e.g., confronting a friend who has been engaging in unhealthy behavior).

Consider the definitions just offered.

Internal Locus of Control:	**External Locus of Control:**
What do you want in this situation?	What do others want you to do?
I want _____.	They want _____.
I want _____.	They want _____.
I want _____.	They want _____.

As you read through your statements, from which direction do you see yourself being guided? Place an X on the following continuum to reflect where you are in relation to the type of control that is most strongly influencing your decisions. Identify the specific forces that you feel are most powerful in your decision making.

Internal _____ **External**

← Student Quotes

I have always believed that a healthy level of achievement is when you are trying your best and pushing your limits at a mildly uncomfortable level. Once you stretch slightly beyond your capacity, you will never shrink back to before. This level of achievement may not necessarily align with society's norms, but that does not matter.

Achievement is reached when one strives to do their best each day, on each task, and to become the best person they can in this world . . . Achievement is based upon each person's personal best. And as long as what they do is their absolute best, then that to me, is achievement.

A healthy level of achievement is when a student gets rewarded for their work and is able to handle that work. It is unhealthy when the achievement is to the detriment of the student by taking too much time or causing undue stress.

I think that every student is different. I do believe that one should not only excel academically but should excel in their personal life as well. Get involved in something that interests you. Take roles that are to your capability level and push those roles to their max.

Too often do we fall into this paradigm that achievement is measured by grades and resume. My view staunchly differs.

A person is achieving at a satisfactory level when, at the end of each day, they can sit down and ask themselves the question: Was I productive today? Am I satisfied with what I did today? If a person is satisfied with their achievements each and every day, this is a healthy level.

[Achievement means] setting goals that are feasible and some that are not as feasible, in order to stay motivated but still bettering oneself . . . pushing the envelope.

ADDITIONAL RESOURCES

Books

Allen, D. (2002). *Getting it done: The art of stress-free productivity.* New York: Penguin.

Boyatzis, R., & McKee, A. (2005). *Resonant leadership.* Cambridge, MA: Harvard Business School Press.

Covey, S. R. (1994). *First things first: To live, to love, to learn, to leave a legacy.* New York: Fireside.

Csikszentmihalyi, M. (1990). *Flow: The psychology of optimal experience.* New York: Harper-Row.

Dweck, C. (2007). *Mindset: The new psychology of success.* New York: Ballantine.

Wilson, S. B., & Dobson, M. S. (2008). *Goal setting: How to create an action plan and achieve your goals* (2nd ed.). New York: AMACOM.

Websites

Locus of Control Test, www.discoveryhealth.queendom.com/questions/lc_short_1.html

McClelland's Motivation Theory, http://www.businessballs.com/davidmcclelland.htm

Taking Control of Our Lives: The Far-Reaching Effects of Locus of Control, www.units.muohio.edu/psybersite/control/index.shtml

What Is Your Locus of Control? www.inst.sfcollege.edu/~mwehr/psyclab/9MotEmoL.htm

12

Optimism

← Focus

Optimism is about being positive. Emotionally intelligent leaders demonstrate a healthy, positive outlook and display a positive regard for the future. Optimism is a powerful force that many overlook. When demonstrated effectively, optimism is contagious and spreads throughout a group or organization. In fact, optimism may be a learned skill—the more often we are able to see the positive, work to identify the best, and encourage others to be better, the more we can produce those results. With optimism, we focus on the best possible outcome, and as such, we align our thoughts in that way and work toward achieving that outcome. Research has found that being optimistic is an important element of emotional intelligence and leadership (Avolio & Luthans, 2006; Goleman, Boyatzis, & McKee, 2002).

← Learning Objectives

- To understand how optimism can be a learned behavior
- To enhance personal perspectives on the power of perception

- To learn how to demonstrate optimistic thinking rather than pessimistic thinking
- To practice optimism as it relates to every day life

REFERENCES

Avolio, B., & Luthans, F. (2006). *The high impact leader*. New York: McGraw Hill.

Goleman, D., Boyatzis, R., & McKee, A. (2002). *Primal leadership: Realizing the power of emotional intelligence*. Boston: Harvard Business School Press.

Optimism
Module 16, Activity 1: Assess Your Family

By Cathy Onion

Think about your family members (parents, grandparents, siblings) and close friends. Decide which characteristic they generally display and write their names in the appropriate column.

Optimistic

_____

_____

_____

_____

_____

_____

Pessimistic

_____

_____

_____

_____

_____

_____

What statements do you often hear the optimists make? How do these statements impact those around them? You?

What statements do you often hear the pessimists make? How do these statements impact those around them? You?

Optimism
Module 17, Activity 2: Putting Optimism into Practice

By Diana Wilson

Optimism is often understood as a reflection of how we view the world. Consider the following two different ways to view the same situation—taking an exam:

- I will never be prepared enough to do well on the exam. (Pessimistic statement)
- I know I am smart and will do my best on the exam. (Optimistic statement)

Rewrite the following statements to reflect an optimistic view.

1. It seems like I put myself in the same unhealthy situations over and over. I will never learn.
   Optimistic:

2. This game is too difficult to learn. I will never figure out how to play it well.
   Optimistic:

3. This event is going to fail. We are really unprepared and no one is doing their part.
   Optimistic:

4. I won't ever find someone to share my life with.
   Optimistic:

5. We have always done things this way. We can't change the process now.
Optimistic:

6. I am too stressed out to get anything done.
Optimistic:

7. Why should I put more effort into this class? The teacher doesn't like me.
Optimistic:

8. I can't make it to the meeting. I'm too busy.
Optimistic:

9. We have ruined so much of our environment. What is the point of being "green" now?
Optimistic:

10. I don't see how this plan can possibly succeed.
Optimistic:

Optimism
Module 17, Activity 3: Food for Thought

By Diana Wilson

Reprinted with permission from *Funny Times*, PO Box 18530, Cleveland Heights, OH 44118.

The following thoughts reflect different perspectives on optimism. Which ones resonate with you?

> While we may not be able to control all that happens to us, we can control what happens inside us.
> —Benjamin Franklin

> An optimist sees an opportunity in every calamity; a pessimist sees a calamity in every opportunity.
> —Winston Churchill

> Optimism is the faith that leads to achievement. Nothing can be done without hope and confidence.
> —Helen Keller

> As we look ahead into the next century, leaders will be those who empower others.
> —Bill Gates

Every person has the power to make others happy.
Some do it simply by entering a room—
others by leaving the room.
Some individuals leave trails of gloom;
others, trails of joy.
Some leave trails of hate and bitterness
others, trails of love and harmony.
Some leave trails of cynicism and pessimism;
others, trails of faith and optimism.
Some leave trails of criticism and resignation;
others trails of gratitude and hope.
What kind of trails do you leave?
—William Arthur Ward

1. When might it be helpful to adopt one of these quotes on optimism? Describe that situation here.

2. Think about someone who you think would benefit from seeing one of these quotes on optimism. Take the time to share it with them and talk with them about how adopting this view or idea might be helpful. How did you benefit from this conversation?

To learn more about optimism, visit:
http://www.authentichappiness.sas.upenn.edu.

✦ Case Study: Optimism, or Lack Thereof

MBA candidate

Steve is the president of the Accounting Association. He is seen as the smartest in the senior class, as he has the highest grade point average. He has a full-time job offer with Big Four Accounting Firm (BFAF), an international firm that is well known and respected in the business world. Steve had an internship with BFAF the fall semester of his junior year. He works hard to get the grades that he has earned, but he does so secretly. Steve does not do much in his free time besides study accounting; he has friends, but he does not hang out with them often. Regardless, everyone knows that Steve is the best accounting student, so people ask him to study with them. Steve is confident that he knows the material and feels that although he does not need to study with a group of people, as the president of the accounting association it is his obligation.

Within the Accounting Association the vice president is Frank and the treasurer is Hank. Frank and Hank are known and loved by all. They are easygoing and fun to hang out with. They spend their weekends having fun, joking and laughing with friends. Frank and Hank are not the smartest students and have little idea of where they're heading, but they are active in the Accounting Association. They attend every meeting with an infectious enthusiasm that is a bit much for some members.

To their credit, Frank and Hank have both taken their positions seriously and have facilitated many changes for the better. Using their social skills, they have reached out to alumni who have donated money for scholarships, and they have attracted potential employers to interview members for jobs and internships.

To graduate, Frank and Hank need to pass the most difficult accounting course on campus—Advanced Financial Accounting Methods. Steve is also in this class. It is a week before the final, and all three are studying. Frank and Hank know that Steve understands the material, so they ask him if they can all study in a group. Frank and Hank look to Steve as a leader: president of the Accounting Association, the smartest student among their friends, and the go-to person if they don't understand a concept. Steve has already been studying for the past two weeks and really understands the material. In reality, he does not need to study with Frank and Hank, but he agrees to do so out of a sense of obligation.

The three meet in a quiet spot in the library and get set up. They start with the first review problem, then work their way through the rest of the problems. All three start the problems at the same time. Steve has done the problems twice before, so he breezes through the questions while Frank and Hank struggle. Steve does not understand why they don't understand it as he does; he gets annoyed with every question they ask. Frank and Hank begin to talk about how hard this test is going to be. Steve joins in with his view that it will be "impossible" and that he will be lucky to get a "B." While Steve waits for the other two to finish, he starts talking about the upcoming baseball season and the movie *Good Will Hunting*. All three get off topic, because *Good Will Hunting* was on television the night before and it's Frank's favorite movie. Steve suggests looking up Matt Damon on Facebook.

Before long, two hours have passed and they've not completed their work because Steve keeps thinking of different things to do on Facebook. Frank and Hank get frustrated because Steve does not want to stay on topic. Then Steve begins to get worried because he sees how hard Frank and Hank are trying. Steve also realizes that on a particular day that he missed class, Frank and Hank were there. He starts asking them questions to learn what the professor said about the final that day in class. Frank and Hank bring up topics that Steve has not spent time on, so he begins to become more and more nervous. To cover his fears, Steve downplays the new information and suggests that the professor probably won't ask those problems, even though he thinks that in all likelihood the professor could (and probably will) test them on that material.

Hank brings up a new topic that neither Steve nor Frank have looked over. Frank wants to slowly walk through the problem and talk about it, even though it is difficult. Steve says "If that's on the test I'm screwed," but he doesn't want to go over it. Frank and Hank start to get down on themselves, thinking that if Steve doesn't think he'll do well, clearly *they* will not do well.

Now it is the day before the test. Frank and Hank have more or less wasted three days trying to study with Steve. Steve essentially brought nothing to the group and wasted Frank and Hank's time. Frank and Hank decide to not study with Steve on the last day, and they get twice as much work done in less than half the time.

After the test, all three meet in the hallway, and Steve immediately blurts out that the exam may have been the hardest test he has ever taken and that he hopes for a big curve. Frank and Hank are mentally exhausted. In the end, Steve got a 98 percent on the "hardest" test he had ever taken, while Frank and Hank barely pass the class, getting scores in the 60-percent range.

Questions:

1. How did Steve, as the leader, bring down the group with his attitude?
2. Should Frank and Hank have studied with Steve in the first place? Do you believe they would have gotten a higher grade if just the two of them had studied together for four days?
3. How could Frank and Hank have told Steve to stop being so negative about the test?
4. What do you think will happen with Steve? Will he learn to work with a team or will he tend to hide in his cubicle by himself because he believe everyone else is not as smart as he is?

5. While Steve thinks he is smarter than both Frank and Hank, how successful do you think he'll be if he tries to get to the top by himself?

✦ Student Quotes

Optimism is, oftentimes, great for organizations, groups, teams, and offices. However, sometimes too much optimism turns people away.

Optimism can allow an organization to keep plugging away at a large project and know that, although overwhelming now, things will be fine in the end. I have also seen optimism leave groups high and dry because they expected things to fall in place . . .

Optimism plays a big role in how a group functions. I am part of our school's hybrid vehicle team, and when we feel like we have the competitive edge, we act quickly and rationally. When we feel like we won't succeed in competition, it takes us a long time to make a decision and even longer to complete a task.

ADDITIONAL RESOURCES

Books

Fox, M. J. (2009). *Always looking up: The adventures of an incurable optimist.* New York: Hyperion.

Glickman, R. (2002). *Optimal thinking: How to be your best self.* San Francisco: Jossey-Bass.

Klein, S. (2006). *The science of happiness: How our brains make us happy—and what we can do to get happier.* Philadelphia, PA: DaCapo Press.

Pollan, S. M., & Levine, M. (2005). *It's all in your head: Thinking your way to happiness.* New York: HarperCollins.

Seligman, M. E. (2006). *Learned optimism: How to change your mind and your life.* New York: Vintage.

Websites

Dr. Martin Seligman, Director of the Positive Psychology Center, University of Pennsylvania and founder of Positive Psychology, www.authentichappiness.sas.upenn.edu.

D'Arcy Vanderpool, Institute for Happiness Studies, Center for Relationship Happiness, www.happinesscoach.com.

13

Initiative

↙ Focus

Showing initiative, in the context of emotionally intelligent leadership, means wanting and seeking opportunities. Emotionally intelligent leaders understand and take initiative. Emotionally intelligent leaders have to both see the opportunity for change *and* make it happen. Demonstrating initiative means that individuals take action and help the work of the group move forward. Initiative requires self-understanding—knowing what you care about, what you are interested in doing, and believing that you can accomplish what you set out to do. Self-confidence and assertiveness are both essential components of initiative. Demonstrating initiative requires both stepping up and speaking out. To find new opportunities, you must know how to look for them and must truly want to make that change happen. Demonstrating initiative means that you take action. In his video *The Power of Vision* (1991), futurist Joel Barker suggests, "Vision without action is merely a dream. Action without vision just passes time. Vision with action changes the world."

Initiative combines thinking about possibilities, imagining a potential direction or action, and making it happen.

✦ Learning Objectives

- To explore the challenges of demonstrating initiative
- To reflect on personal experiences of demonstrating initiative
- To identify the connections between teamwork and initiative

REFERENCE

Barker, J. (1991). *The power of vision* (VHS). United States: Starthrower Distribution.

Initiative
Module 18, Activity 1: Goal Reached

By Anthony Middlebrooks

At the top of the time line presented here, write the conclusion of a project or effort that you successfully completed. Along the line, indicate major steps you took toward accomplishing this goal. On the left side, describe each major step. On the right side, write the things you did to accomplish each step (specific tasks), including who you talked to, what you did, and what went right and/or wrong along the way.

As you look at these steps and what you did, what did you do best? What could have been improved?

What feelings emerged as these steps were accomplished?

How much initiative would you say you took in making the goal happen?

✦ Case Study: Kick It In or Kick Him Out?

Kristyn Riemer

The Shore View Country Club (SVCC) in northern Idaho is currently celebrating its hundred-year anniversary. SVCC includes an eighteen-hole golf course, tennis courts, and an outdoor pool. The clubhouse has dining facilities and banquet rooms for private events. The country club provides social activities for its members such as dinner dances, date nights, holiday parties, clam bakes, golf tournaments, and swim meets.

SVCC is staffed by a general manager, an assistant general manager, a food and beverage director, a dining room manager, an event director, and a wait staff of about twenty. The club has a culinary department, an accounting department, and a maintenance department. The food and beverage director, Chevy, and the dining room manager, Rodney, work together to organize and execute dinners and social functions. As the person who directly reports to the general managers, Chevy has many responsibilities. He must order food and beverage ingredients for the culinary department, ensure that each event is set up and executed properly, and delegate tasks to the servers and bartenders.

On a daily basis, Chevy arrives at work later than all of the other managers. Although there is no official arrival time, it is considered acceptable to arrive any time before noon, as club events usually run until late in the evening. Chevy, however, usually arrives between 2:00 and 3:00 PM. Chevy's coworkers, particularly Rodney, become aggravated because they cannot rely on him for extra help or to follow through on necessary tasks. During weekly staff meetings, Chevy is usually unprepared, coming without his calendar or a notepad. In addition, he rarely stays on the subject at hand. Instead of keeping the conversation to work-related topics, he makes jokes and sarcastic remarks. When discussing what should be done for a particular event, Chevy does not offer an answer or suggestion until someone else makes a decision for him. In such cases, his reactions may be constructive or unproductive, depending on his mood.

Chevy has an "I come first" mentality. During busy hours or in the middle of important events, he may be found watching the "big game" on television or playing on the computer in his office. He seems to hide from situations in which he would have to make important decisions. During these times, the wait staff must use their own discretion when problems or questions arise. In many situations, Chevy holds a leadership position but does not "do" leadership. For example, one of Chevy's responsibilities is to ensure that each event is set up properly the day before it occurs; however, Chevy usually relies on the other managers to point him in the right direction. Instead of deciding on seating arrangements and how to set up the event, or delegating small tasks to each employee, Chevy asks, "What do you think we should do?"

Chevy's behavior has caused his subordinates to lose trust in him and forced Rodney to cover for him on many occasions. Because Rodney and Chevy work so closely together on events, Chevy's subordinates often bring their questions to Rodney. Rodney feels overwhelmed and aggravated because he has to take care of his own responsibilities as well as Chevy's. Even though Chevy displays optimism and has the ability to develop relationships, all his shortcomings detailed here overshadow his strengths.

Questions:
1. How does Chevy's lack of initiative affect his subordinates? His colleague Rodney?
2. What would happen if Chevy's lack of initiative "infected" the other employees?
3. How could the other managers, specifically Rodney, help Chevy improve his leadership skills?

4. How do the general manager and assistant general manager figure into this scenario?

5. In general, how important is initiative in a teamwork setting?

✦ Student Quotes

Initiative comes in many forms. Sometimes it is as simple as doing your homework, but more often it is expressed through stepping up to the plate and taking on a task that no one else will. This can be planning an event, confronting someone, or speaking out for an ideal. Initiative can motivate others as well.

Leaders have initiative. She is the person who takes charge, takes on a little more in the group, and takes a position within an organization that requires more work.

There needs to be the catalyst for change, and sometimes it is someone who stands above the rest and says, "Let's do this," that initiates the change . . .

Students who take initiative tend to be the students who see positive results in a relatively small amount of time.

When students take initiative, it is much more likely that they will succeed in their endeavors. When a task is forced upon them, students often lack the motivation and initiative to complete the objective. No one wants to do what they have to do; they want to do what they want to do.

ADDITIONAL RESOURCES

Allen, D. (2001). *Getting things done: The art of stress-free productivity.* New York: Penguin Books.

Cooper, R. K., & Sawaf, A. (1996). *Executive EQ: Emotional intelligence in leadership and organizations.* New York: Perigee Books.

Fishel, R. (2003). *Change almost anything in 21 days: Recharge your life with the power of over 500 affirmations.* Deerfield Beach, FL: Health Communications.

Fisher, R., & Sharp, A. (1998). *Getting it done: How to lead when you're not in charge.* New York: HarperBusiness.

14

Consciousness of Others

❖ **Focus**

Demonstrating consciousness of others means being aware of and attuned to those with whom you are working. Leadership is not a solo activity—it's based on relationships. Whether you think of a traditional leader-follower relationship or something more like a group of collaborators, the relationship among the people involved is essential. Consciousness of others includes the ability to empathize, inspire, influence, and coach. Teamwork, dealing with conflict and differences, and learning how to work effectively with others to bring about change are all essential capacities of emotionally intelligent leadership. Because the setting and situation for leadership changes so often, many variables affect leadership. Therefore it's essential that leaders learn how to work with others and incorporate them effectively in the leadership equation.

❖ **Learning Objectives**

- To introduce the range of specific capacities that make up consciousness of others

- To reflect on a set of familiar individuals and identify their similarities and differences
- To begin to develop an analytical framework for enhancing consciousness of others

Consciousness of Others
Module 19, Activity 1: Working with Others

By Marcy Levy Shankman and Scott J. Allen

On the following list, check the three capacities you think are most important for effective leadership.

__*Empathy*: Understanding others from their perspective

__*Citizenship*: Recognizing and fulfilling your responsibility for others or the group

__*Inspiration*: Motivating and moving others toward a shared vision

__*Influence*: Demonstrating skills of persuasion

__*Coaching*: Helping others enhance their skills and abilities

__*Change agent*: Seeking out and working with others toward new directions

__*Conflict management*: Identifying and resolving problems and issues with others

__*Developing relationships*: Creating connections between, among, and with people

__*Teamwork*: Working effectively with others in a group

__*Capitalizing on differences*: Building on assets that come from differences with others

After a group activity, reflect on the following:

1. Why are the three capacities you chose the most relevant to you?

(Continued)

2. What happens when one of these capacities is overused? Why?

3. What happens if the other capacities (the ones you didn't check) are ignored? What is lost?

Reference

Shankman, M. L., & Allen, S. J. (2008). *Emotionally intelligent leadership: A guide for college students*. San Francisco: Jossey-Bass.

Consciousness of Others
Module 19, Activity 2: Who Do I Know?

By Marcy Levy Shankman and Scott J. Allen

Think about people you know well and complete the following chart. First identify what is similar and different about them as you consider their talents, interests, and personalities. As a second step, think about yourself in relation to the people you've listed. Circle at least one similarity or difference between you and each person.

Person	Similarities	Differences

1. When might it be helpful for you to call on each of these people?

2. When would someone on the list not be helpful?

✦ Student Quotes

I can really respect when the leader gets to know the "followers."

A leader is someone who engages the members of the group, trusts them, and monitors and supports their progress, and throughout the entire process brings a sense of excitement and joy to the job/project.

People are more likely to believe in a person and respect someone who recognizes and fulfills responsibilities to others. People are also more likely to follow such a leader because they believe this person to be someone who truly has an interest in the people.

It is essential that leaders take the time to think about and feel for their followers. If something the leader does upsets the followers, this can be detrimental to the leader's cause, and therefore, should not be taken lightly.

A leader must understand what others are going through; however, becoming too empathetic can lead to being undermined in a way. By being too lax and too empathetic you can allow people to get away with not doing their share.

ADDITIONAL RESOURCES

Bolton, R., & Bolton, D. G. (2009). *People styles at work . . . and beyond: Making bad relationships good and good relationships better*. New York: AMACOM.

Covey, S.M.R. (2008). *The speed of trust: The one thing that changes everything*. New York: Free Press.

Maxwell, J. C. (2004). *Relationships 101*. Nashville, TN: Thomas Nelson.

Straus, D., & Layton, T. C. (2002). *How to make collaboration work: Powerful ways to build consensus, solve problems, and make decisions*. San Francisco: Berrett-Koehler.

15

Empathy

✦ Focus

Empathy is about understanding others from their perspective. Emotionally intelligent leadership and, more specifically, the capacity of empathy, are about perceiving the emotions of others. When leaders display empathy, they have the opportunity to build healthier relationships, manage difficult situations, and develop trust more effectively. Being empathetic requires an individual to have a high level of self-awareness as well as awareness of others. The cliché "put yourself in someone else's shoes" truly defines the capacity of empathy, because to identify with the emotions of another person, you must first understand your own emotions. Learning how to recognize and name your emotions (some call this emotional literacy) is an essential stepping stone for demonstrating empathy.

✦ Learning Objectives

- To increase your understanding of the concept of empathy
- To practice active listening skills
- To learn the difference between listening for feelings and listening for perspective

Empathy
Module 20, Activity 1: Practice Your Skills

By Ginny Carroll

Empathy requires the ability to understand how others perceive situations based on their values and beliefs about the world. Consider the following quote:

> Leadership is about empathy. It is about having the ability to relate and to connect with people for the purpose of inspiring and empowering their lives.
> —Oprah Winfrey

What does this quote mean to you?

Exercise

Initiate two different conversations to practice your skills of empathetic listening. In these conversations, you will be listening intently to others for two important messages being communicated— feelings and context.

- *Conversation #1:* Ask someone to share with you a recent experience that was difficult or challenging for them. Your role is to listen for the person's feelings. To that end:
  - Listen for and speak only to the emotions being expressed by the speaker.
  - Do not attempt to solve the speaker's problem. Offer a mirror (reflection) in which the person can better see the situation and hear what emotions they are expressing.
  - Ask questions that help the speaker clarify his or her feelings.

- *Conversation #2:* Ask someone to share with you a recent experience that was either challenging or exciting. Listen for the speaker's context. Context involves many variables including perspective, the situation and setting of the experience, and what happened. Your role is to:
  - Pay attention to what the speaker says about the setting, situation, and his or her perspective on the experience.
  - Ask questions that will help the speaker better understand the background and events of the experience.

Empathy
Module 20, Activity 2: Reflection

By Ginny Carroll

After completing Activity 1, consider the following questions and write your responses in the space provided.

1. Which was harder for you to identify—feelings or context?

2. How did the speaker respond when your reflection was accurate for the speaker's feelings? How does this link with the previous question?

3. How often did you want to interrupt and add your own feelings to the conversation? How did you feel about not interrupting? If you did interrupt, what do you think the effect was?

4. What questions did you ask to get to the speaker's feelings?

5. What questions did you ask to clarify the speaker's context?

✦ Case Study: When the Leader Lacks Empathy

Bryan Gacka

Delta Gamma Theta (DGT) fraternity is a long-standing and popular student organization at Eastern State University. It has a reputation of excellence in service, academics, and athletics. The fraternity's primary mission is to foster and promote brotherhood among its members.

The executive council governs the fraternity; it's comprised of the president, vice president, and treasurer, and the directors of programming and recruitment. A separate judicial board (JB) serves to enforce the fraternity bylaws and hears any cases of violations that come before it. The JB plays an important role because it is entrusted with ensuring that decisions comply with the rules and that brothers continually meet the criteria for membership.

Dave is one of the most popular fraternity members. He is charismatic, outgoing, and willing to help a brother in need. He holds one of the fraternity's highest grade point averages and regularly attends its social and service events. Although he hasn't held an official position yet, many see him as eventually being elected president.

Mark, another member of the fraternity, is the head of the judicial board. He is known for his dedication to the fraternity. Although Mark remains fair and impartial during judicial hearings, he can be severe at times. Mark's position and expertise afford him a great deal of influence over other JB members, the executive council, and fraternity members. Mark and Dave are friendly with one another, but they do not spend a great deal of time together.

In recent weeks, many members have noticed a dramatic change in Dave. He has been absent from many fraternity events, including missing four consecutive weekly fraternity chapter meetings. It is rumored that his grades have begun to suffer due to poor class attendance. Dave's general demeanor seems to be different as well. He has become reserved and guarded when interacting with brothers, and he has turned down many requests for help.

Following his fourth chapter meeting absence, Mark calls Dave before the JB. Missing four chapter meetings is a violation of the bylaws. Additionally, midterm grades have just been released, and Dave's grades indicate he may fall below the fraternity's minimum standards when the semester concludes. One concerned member, Stephen approaches Dave prior to the judicial hearing to learn what has caused the dramatic change.

After a lengthy discussion, Dave finally opens up to Stephen as to why he has been acting differently. At the beginning of the semester, Dave's parents notified him that they were getting a divorce. The news blindsided him, creating an emotional and stressful situation. Dave was so shaken that he withdrew from many of his normal activities and also found himself spending a great deal of time with his younger brother, who was upset over the divorce. Dave had not told anyone of the situation because he "did not want to be a burden."

Stephen communicates this information to the rest of the fraternity. When the judicial hearing commences, Mark asks Dave for an explanation for his chapter absences and poor academic performance. Dave explains about the divorce and assures the JB that he is beginning to cope with the situation in healthier ways.

Despite this knowledge, Mark shows little empathy for Dave. He has not experienced a divorce in his family, and he has trouble understanding why Dave's behavior changed so dramatically. Mark does not believe Dave's actions were appropriate or his explanation adequate.

During deliberation, Mark communicates his opinions of Dave's situation to the JB members. Most of them feel Dave should not be punished, due to the extenuating circumstances of his parents' divorce. They see the situation from Dave's perspective and understand why he has acted in such a manner.

Mark, on the other hand, cannot put himself in Dave's shoes. He feels Dave has been making excuses for his actions rather than acknowledging them. Mark does not feel that Dave's absences and poor academic performance are a result of his coping with his parents' divorce. After all, Mark reasons, why would Dave not seek support from his fellow fraternity brothers in this difficult time? Mark feels that, had Dave done so, he would have reacted in a completely different manner.

After much debate, the JB reaches a majority decision to place Dave on probation. Mark convinces enough of the JB that Dave's behavior is due not to the divorce but rather to a general lack of concern for the fraternity. Although it is unfortunate that Dave's parents are getting a divorce, Mark is sure that this had no bearing on Dave's absences.

Questions:

1. How does Mark's lack of empathy for Dave's situation affect his decision?
2. How important is it for a person in Mark's leadership position to possess empathy? Why?
3. How might the decision to place Dave on probation affect both Dave and the fraternity?
4. How best could fraternity members approach and aid Mark to help him learn to use empathy in the future?

✦ Student Quotes

Too much empathy will slow the group down tremendously. A leader can't make everyone happy. Everyone should be heard and feedback should be given when unrealistic solutions are shared.

➤◆

Empathy is understanding the situation and how it affects the person. Leadership is helping to guide them through the situation without solving it for them.

Empathy is necessary to truly understand the people one wishes to lead.

I think empathy is a key component to effective leadership. It is essential that leaders take the time to think about and feel for their followers. If something the leader does upsets the followers, this can be detrimental to the leader's cause, and therefore should not be taken lightly.

Empathy helps leaders show members they care. Empathy allows leaders to be available and supportive . . . but if they are too empathetic they can be taken advantage of and ruled by their emotions.

ADDITIONAL RESOURCES

Baron-Cohen, S. (2004). *The essential difference: Men, women, and the extreme brain.* New York: Penguin Books.

Brady, M. (2003). *The wisdom of listening.* Somerville, MA: Wisdom Publications.

Ekman, P. (2007). *Emotions revealed: Recognizing faces and feelings to improve communication and emotional life* (2nd ed.). New York: Owl Books.

Hartley, G., & Karinch, M. (2007). *I can read you like a book: How to spot messages and emotions people are really sending with their body language.* Franklin Lakes, NJ: Career Press.

Selby, J. (2007). *Listening with empathy: Creating genuine connections with customers and colleagues.* Charlottesville, VA: Hampton Roads.

16

Citizenship

✦ Focus

Citizenship, as a capacity of emotionally intelligent leadership, reflects our ability to recognize and fulfill our responsibility for others or the group. Emotionally intelligent leaders must be aware of what it means to be a part of something bigger than themselves. An essential component is to fulfill the ethical and moral obligations inherent in the values of the community. As a result, emotionally intelligent leaders know when to give of themselves for the benefit of others and the larger group. Demonstrating emotionally intelligent leadership requires us to recognize that being involved in a group is not a solo, self-oriented act. "To be a good citizen is to work for positive change on behalf of others and the community" (Higher Education Research Institute, 1996, p. 23). Citizenship also implies the broader concept of interdependence. When you demonstrate citizenship, you give of yourself and see yourself as responsible both for and to others. Interdependence, collaboration, and working effectively with others for the good of the organization or cause reflects the demands of leadership in the twenty-first century (Knapp, 2006).

✦ Learning Objectives

- To enhance your understanding of what citizenship means and where it is evident
- To explore how leadership and citizenship behaviors happen at all levels of an organization or group
- To understand why citizenship behaviors may not be demonstrated and how to increase the likelihood that they are
- To develop an action statement that reflects a personal commitment to demonstrate citizenship

REFERENCE

Higher Education Research Institute (1996). *A social change model of leadership development: Guidebook version III*. Los Angeles: University of California Los Angeles Higher Education Research Institute.

Knapp, J. C. (Ed.). (2006). *For the common good: The ethics of leadership in the 21st century*. New York: Praeger.

Citizenship
Module 21, Activity 1: Formal Democracy versus Living Democracy: An Argument

By Jon Dooley

Please read the following passage:

Voice One: Democracy is one form of government, pure and simple. It depends on some key institutions: elected leadership, more than one party, and a balance of power. In the case of the United States, that means three branches of government.

Voice Two: But lots of countries have impressive institutions of democracy and still the majority of citizens live in misery. To work, democracy has to be more. It has to be a way of life—a way of life that involves the values and practices people engage in daily in all aspects of their public lives.

Voice One: Sure, it depends on some practices. The citizen has to vote, for example; the public official has to be honest. But the great thing about democracy is precisely that it doesn't require very much from citizens, leaving them free to pursue their private lives. That's what really matters to people.

Voice Two: Citizenship is a lot more than voting. And our public lives are much more than just our ties to government. Politicians are not the only people who live in a public world. Every one of us lives in a public world. But our public lives are rewarding—for ourselves and our society—to the extent that we have a real say in the workplace, at school, in the community, in relation to the media, and to human services, as well as in government.

Voice One: But democracy isn't about what goes on in the workplace or school. These institutions are *protected* by democratic government, but they certainly aren't the same thing as democracy. Furthermore, your ideas turn ordinary people into decision makers. Democracy works best when people elect *others* who are better qualified to keep the machinery of government running smoothly.

Voice Two: Citizens ought to determine the values upon which the decision makers act. It's these so-called experts—people who

(*Continued*)

are supposed to be better qualified—who have gotten us into the mess we're in now! Experts don't have to be *on top* making the choices. Instead, they ought to be *on tap* to citizens who are choosing the directions our society ought to go in.

Voice One: But most people don't want to be involved. Public life is no picnic. It's nasty and getting nastier all the time. In a democracy, public life is a necessary evil. We minimize the nuisance by minimizing government—and by assigning public roles to others, to officials, in order to protect our private freedom.

Voice Two: But in reality there are millions of regular people discovering the *rewards* of public life at school, at work, and in the community. They are discovering that their voices *do* count. They're building strengths they didn't know they had—to communicate, to make decisions, to solve problems. Some are even discovering the *fun* of power!

Voice One: You've blurred some important distinctions. People you're talking about may be building their *character* through good works, but all that's required for *citizenship* is responsible voting—electing the best people to run our government.

Voice Two: Democracy requires a lot more of us than being intelligent voters. It requires that we learn to solve problems with others—that we learn to listen, to negotiate, and to evaluate. To think and speak effectively. To go beyond simple protest in order to wield power, becoming partners in problem solving. This isn't about so-called good work; it's about our vital interests. And it isn't about simply running our government; it's about running our *lives.*

Voice One: But what you're saying about the way it *ought* to be is irrelevant. Americans are apathetic.

Voice Two: No, Americans aren't apathetic. Study after study shows they're angry. Angry about being shut out of decision making. Angry that their democracy's been stolen from them.

Voice One: Our democracy hasn't been stolen. It's still in place. It's been in place for over two hundred years!

Voice Two: Democracy is never fully in place. It is always in flux, a work in progress. Democracy is dynamic. It evolves in response to the creative action of citizens. It's what we make of it.

Questions

- Think back over the last year. Where have you heard or read any of these arguments?

- Which voice in this dialogue best matches your own views? In what ways?

- What are some of the influences in your life—people, institutions, or experiences—that have shaped your views?

- What is the responsibility of leaders to engage a broad range of citizens or members in problem solving?

- What is the responsibility of average citizens or members in problem solving?

Reference

Lappé, F. M., & Du Bois, P. M. (1994). *The quickening of America: Rebuilding our nation, remaking our lives*. San Francisco: Jossey-Bass.

Citizenship
Module 22, Activity 2: Citizenship in Our Organizations

By John Shertzer

Consider a group or organization in which you're involved. Write the name here:

_____

In the table, fill in behaviors or actions that would constitute minimal, good, and exemplary citizenship for each of the categories. In the far right column, rate your own level of citizenship for each category.

Category	Constitutes minimal citizenship	Constitutes good citizenship	Constitutes exemplary citizenship	Self-rating
Attendance at meetings				
Participation in meetings				
Recruiting new members				
Participation in committees				

Category	Constitutes minimal citizenship	Constitutes good citizenship	Constitutes exemplary citizenship	Self-rating
Seeking elected officer positions				
Attendance at organization's events				
Public relations / promotions for organization				
Representing the organization externally				
Dues or financial commitments				
Fundraising activities				
Volunteering for tasks/duties				
Other				

Citizenship
Module 22, Activity 3: Falling Short of Expectations

By John Shertzer

List reasons for why group members have difficulty meeting expectations.

What can you do to influence the level of citizenship being demonstrated?

List what you consider to be the top five steps for influencing the level of citizenship in a group.

1. _____

2. _____

3. _____

4. _____

5. _____

✦ Student Quotes

When members fulfill their duty, the entire aura of the organization is positive.

When a person sees that they have done their part in accomplishing a goal for the group, there is a joy inside them. Responsibility is important and not handled well by some.

I believe that there comes a point in an individual's life when he realizes that satisfaction does not simply result from making yourself happy. It results from interactions with others and fulfilling their needs. When this occurs, a group runs more efficiently.

People are more likely to believe in a person and respect someone who recognizes and fulfills responsibilities to others. People are also more likely to follow such a leader because they believe this person to be someone who truly has an interest in the people and can be trusted.

There is nothing to be seen when a responsibility is recognized and fulfilled. To the average member, it appears that the gears of the organization are turning on their own. Something is only noticed when the ball is dropped.

ADDITIONAL RESOURCES

Eisenhower Leadership Program Grant (1995). *Citizens of change program: Application guidebook for the social change model of leadership development.* De Pere, WI: Citizen Leadership Development Center, St. Norbert College.

Loeb, P. R. (1999). *Soul of a citizen: Living with conviction in a cynical time.* New York: St. Martin's Press.

Moyer, B., McAllister, J., Finley, M. L., & Soifer, S. (2001). *Doing democracy.* Gabriola Island, British Columbia: New Society Publishers.

Payton, R. L., & Moody, M. P. (2008). *Understanding philanthropy: Its meaning and mission.* Bloomington, IN: Indiana University Press.

Shankman, M. L., and Allen, S. J. (2008). *Emotionally intelligent leadership: A guide for college students.* San Francisco: Jossey-Bass.

17

Inspiration

><

Inspiration requires that we motivate and move others toward a shared vision. Being perceived as an inspirational individual by others is an important capacity of emotionally intelligent leadership. Inspiration works through relationships. Effective leadership entails generating feelings of optimism and commitment to organizational goals through individual actions, words, and accomplishments. At times, inspiration is perceived as an ability held by one individual—the leader. In fact, inspiration is a social dynamic that is multidirectional. Although some may think that only charisma generates this feeling in others, inspiration can manifest in many different ways. For instance, some people are great at creating an environment that elicits inspirational acts from group members. Role modeling is another source of inspiration. Likewise, inspiration may come from how ideas are communicated through the leader's behavior. Finally, the quality of relationships both within and outside of the group generates inspiration for many. At the core of inspiration is a person's ability to unleash energy in others and provide direction for it.

← Learning Objectives

- To develop a vision statement for a group or organization
- To learn how to represent a vision in multiple forms of expression
- To connect the work of achieving a vision with a person's motivation
- To explore the connection between inspiration and values

Inspiration
Module 23, Activity 1: Defining Vision

By Henry Parkinson

An effective vision should:

- Take you where you want to go
- Be far reaching, but attainable
- Change and adapt with the environment
- Be something you believe in and have passion for
- Give you direction for the future

Think about a group or organization that is important to you.

List it here: _____

Where do you see this group or organization in three to five years?

What do you want this group/organization to be known for five years from now?

What is your vision statement for this group/organization?

Inspiration 2: Shared Values
Module 24, Activity 2: Inspiration Bingo

By Adam Peck

Fill in as many blanks as possible.

IN	SP	IR	AT	ION
Intrinsically motivated people are motivated: A. Internally B. Externally	Inspiring leaders motivate others through s_____d values.	How is inspiration different from motivation?	Others are more likely to support decisions they disagree with when they are c_____ed about the decision.	If the leader's values do not match those of the people that he or she leads, the leader should . . . (answer below)
Emotionally intelligent leaders use knowledge of s_____ and o_____ to inspire.	Leadership and inspiration are in the eye of the b_____r.	Inspiration is defined as that which motivates and moves others toward a shared v_____.	People support and care about what they help to c_____.	A. Reevaluate . . .
For someone to be inspired, it must connect to their v_____.	Emotionally intelligent leaders know how to encourage those that they lead to motivate th_____s.	FREE SPACE	Values are the principles that guide our a_____.	B. Assess . . .
What is your top value? _____	Emotionally Intelligent leaders a____ rather than g_____ what followers and organizations value.	Extrinsically motivated people are motivated: A. Internally B. Externally	The best way to lead others is to make them feel h_____ and v_____.	C. Find . . .
Remember, you can't be all t_____ to all p_____.	Inspiration is an int_____able quality that can be hard to d_____.	Our values reflect our most important p_____.	We each c_____ to be inspired.	D. Persuade . . .

Inspiration
Module 24, Activity 3: Shared Values

By Adam Peck

What values are most important to you when you serve in a formal or informal leadership role? What values do you think are most important to the group/organization? Complete the following.

Individual Values

From the following, select your *one* top value as it relates to leadership. Many of these values will be important to you, so give it careful thought.

Challenge	Influence	Prosperity
Creativity	Order or Structure	Self-Reliance
Integrity	Power	Significance
Harmony	Progress	Spirituality

Group Values

Now select the value you think will be most important to a group/ organization in which you are a member. If you don't know the group/organization very well, take an educated guess.

Challenge	Influence	Prosperity
Creativity	Order or Structure	Self-Reliance
Integrity	Power	Significance
Harmony	Progress	Spirituality

(*Continued*)

Motivation

Which of the following two motivation preferences better describes you? Remember, both are equally valid. You might begin by asking yourself the following questions: When was the last time I was really motivated? What motivated me? Mark your general preference.

__*Extrinsic*: Extrinsically motivated people are motivated from outside themselves. They tend to be most motivated by recognition, awards, financial rewards, and the appreciation of others.

__*Intrinsic*: Intrinsically motivated people are motivated from within themselves. They tend to be most motivated by a sense of personal pride in accomplishment, achievement of individual goals, or a desire to help others.

✦ Case Study: A True Inspiration—Or Not?

Paul Martin

Habitat for Humanity is a national not-for-profit organization that organizes volunteers and resources for various projects to combat poverty and homelessness. At one local campus, the Habitat for Humanity group performs common yard work and household tasks to help create a more friendly and healthy environment for the community members.

John decided that he wanted to make a difference in his community, so he called Mary, a local leader for Habitat for Humanity, to set up a meeting to discuss how he could become involved. Not only did Mary assume responsibility for helping with Habitat for Humanity, but she also kept a 4.0 grade point average, was part of the student union, and belonged to a sorority on campus. Mary had impeccable credentials; she "looked great on paper." But John came to discover that she seemed to be missing a certain attribute that most true leaders possess: the ability to inspire others.

The first project John volunteered for took place during his sophomore year in college. On a spring weekend, he woke up at 7:00 A.M., which was not easy for him. He met eight other people in the lobby of the residence hall to figure out how to carpool most efficiently for the day. The trouble was, they were missing the ninth person: Mary. She was one of two students who had volunteered to drive, because two of the students did not have a car. She called to say she was on her way and was "running a few minutes late."

By the time Mary arrived, it was 11:30 A.M. On the drive to the house, Mary complained to John and the other student that her alarm did not work correctly and her car would not start. But John had a feeling she was lying; he could smell stale alcohol in the car, most likely lingering from the night before. He was disappointed to hear these excuses from Mary, who presented herself as a leader for Habitat for Humanity. To make matters worse, by the time the three arrived at their destination, they knocked on the door and realized no one was home. Clearly, they were not going to have the chance to volunteer for the rest of the day.

When they got back into the car, Mary began complaining about how they had wasted her day. John refrained from telling Mary how he really felt and how hypocritical he thought she was being. Once back in his room, John sat there and thought about the morning. He had been so excited to help his community, and in the end found himself lying on his bed, not wanting to go back to Habitat for Humanity.

John realized, though, that he was upset not with Habitat but with Mary. He decided Mary was one of the worst leaders he had ever met. In fact, he realized she wasn't a leader at all. Not only did she not inspire him to help, but she actually "uninspired" him. Although she called herself a leader, Mary lacked the ability to inspire people to want to help her or the cause. Her lack of follow-through and her negative attitude reflected poorly on her. John realized that although she was a positional leader on campus, her actions made it clear that she really wasn't one. This reflection helped John see that Mary had almost deprived him of the opportunity to help a truly inspiring organization. He returned to Habitat, this time with a different leader, and enjoyed volunteering throughout the rest of his college years.

Questions:
1. What lessons did John learn about the influence one person can have on an organization? Consider both positive and negative examples from this scenario.
2. How did Mary's attitude and demeanor affect the organization? How did they affect John?
3. How might Mary have been inspirational in her own actions, without changing the facts of the situation?

4. What might John have done differently to remedy the situation with Mary?

Student Quotes

I like leaders who are visionary (have good ideas), optimistic (believe something can get done), and encouraging (appreciate the contributions of the different teammates).

I enjoy honesty and consistency. Leaders who uphold themselves in a manner that I aspire to are an inspiration to me.

As a follower I like someone who will give me specific tasks and guide me, but not try to control exactly what I do. I like to be given something specific but still have the creative freedom to do what I think is best.

[Inspiration is] a style that is both flash and substance. If someone can keep my attention while providing me with a purpose then I will go with them until the project is complete. Direction and energy are what capture me.

As a follower, I am inspired by passionate people–people who aren't afraid to put themselves out there, and work for a change. I am inspired by people who are willing to take risks, and know that not everything will always work out the way they want it to.

What inspires me as a follower is a leader who is willing to jump into the pit with you to dig the organization out of the hole [it has] made.

ADDITIONAL RESOURCES

Leider, R. J. (2005). *The power of purpose: Creating meaning in your life and work*. San Francisco: Berrett-Koehler.

Loeb, P. R. (1999). *Soul of a citizen: Living with conviction in a cynical time*. New York: St. Martin's Griffin.

Razeghi, A. (2006). *Hope: How triumphant leaders create the future*. San Francisco: Jossey-Bass.

Temes, P. S. (2007). *The power of purpose: Living well by doing good*. New York: Three Rivers Press.

Wills, G. (1994). *Certain trumpets: The call of leaders*. New York: Simon & Schuster.

18

Influence

← Focus

The capacity of influence is fundamental to leadership; those who have this capacity demonstrate skills of persuasion. Emotionally intelligent leaders have the ability to persuade others with information, ideas, emotion, behavior, and a strong commitment to organizational values and purpose. They involve others to engage in a process of mutual exploration and action. Regardless of whether you hold a formal or informal position, you have the opportunity to influence. To influence others means that you believe in a desired end enough to share your ideas and create space for others. Having influence means that you effectively persuade others to join your cause, movement, solution, and so forth. This persuasion, as suggested by leadership scholar Bernard Bass (1997), means that you "display conviction; emphasize trust; take stands on different issues; present their most important values; emphasize the importance of purpose, commitment and ethical consequences of decision making" (p. 133).

✦ Learning Objectives

- To learn about different stages of influence
- To identify an area of interest in which influencing others is necessary
- To develop a personal action plan for practicing skills of persuasion

REFERENCE

Bass, B. (1997). Does the transactional-transformational leadership paradigm transcend organizational and national boundaries? *American Psychology*, 52(2), 130–139.

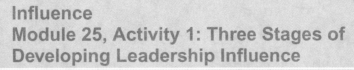

Influence
Module 25, Activity 1: Three Stages of
Developing Leadership Influence

By Gary Manka

Stage 1. Influence must first be developed through personal growth.
Before you can influence others, you must understand and
manage yourself.

*What aspects of your personality do you think need further
development?*

Stage 2. The ability to influence others is a direct result of personal
growth. Personal growth must be expanded to occur outside of
self through social awareness and relationship management.

*What do you need to do to become more aware of others, how
they're feeling, and how you interact with them?*

Stage 3. The ability to influence self and others is also directly
affected by the organizational environment in which we work.
More often than not, the organizations we create can take on
a life of their own and don't work as we had originally planned
them to work.

*Think of an organization to which you belong. How would you
describe the environment of this organization? What aspects of
this organization are unpredictable?*

References

Goleman, D. (1995). *Emotional intelligence*. New York: Bantam Books.

Watkins, M. (2007). "Infectious leadership." *The Leading Edge*. Boston:
Harvard Business Publishing. http://blogs.hbr.org/watkins/2007/10/
infectious_leadership.html

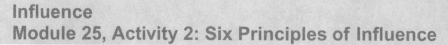

Influence
Module 25, Activity 2: Six Principles of Influence

By Gary Manka

Reciprocation: "We should try to repay, in kind, what another person has provided us" (p. 7).

Commitment and Consistency: "Once we have made a choice or taken a stand, we will encounter personal and interpersonal pressure to behave consistently with that commitment" (p. 57).

Social Proof: "One means we use to determine what is correct is to find out what other people think is correct. We view a behavior as more correct in a given situation to the degree that we see others performing it" (p. 116).

Liking: "We most prefer to say yes to the requests of someone we know and like" (p. 167).

Authority: "We are trained from birth that obedience to proper authority is right and disobedience is wrong" (p. 216).

Scarcity: "Opportunities seem more valuable to us when their availability is limited. In fact, people seem to be more motivated by the thought of losing something than by the thought of gaining something of equal value" (p. 238).

Place a check by the principles that are most obvious to you in your life.

Describe the ways in which you see these principles of influence in action. Think about people whom you consider influential. Which principles do they employ?

Reference

Cialdini, R. B. (2007). *Influence: The psychology of persuasion*. New York: HarperCollins Publishers, Inc.

Influence
Module 25, Activity 3: Developing Personal and Social Influence

By Gary Manka

The following model describes a way to develop your personal and social influence. After each level listed here, write your thoughts on how to complete each level—that is, what can you do to act on each level? Be specific.

Level 1: Learn—Everything from anyone.

Level 2: Perform—Persevere and work continuously hard.

Level 3: Lead—Extend personal abilities by expanding team.

(Continued)

Level 4: Develop Leaders—Find and develop other leaders while speaking truth and developing trust in every interaction.

Level 5: Develop Leaders Who Develop Leaders—Create a legacy that outlives the leader.

Reference

Brady, C., & Woodward, O. (2005). *Launching a leadership revolution: Mastering the five levels of influence*. New York: Business Plus.

Influence
Module 25, Activity 4: Personal Persuasion Action Plan

By Gary Manka

Consider the following ideas related to influence.

1. Learn the rules of influence for a group/organization that you are a part of.

   Describe what works. How do individuals effectively influence others?

   What doesn't seem to work?

2. Determine how these rules may personally affect your actions and decisions. How is leadership affected by the actions and decisions of others?

3. How do you know whether rules benefit you? What are your benchmarks or indicators?

(Continued)

4. Learn to recognize red flags or indicators when these rules are being used on you and how to say *"no"* when needed. What will you do or say when you recognize that the rules are not benefitting you?

Write your responses to the following:

I care about _____
      (an issue, cause, organization, and so on). What do I think about it?

People I know with whom I want to share these thoughts are . . .

Here's a story I want to tell them about it . . .

Here's what I'd like them to think about it . . .

✦ Case Study: Member Apathy in the University Finance Organization

Will Bargar

The University Finance Organization (UFO) has approximately one hundred active undergraduate members who participate in various activities, such as speaker events, throughout the year. The speakers are the main draw for members; a wide range of professionals come to the weekly meetings to offer insight, advice, experience, and opportunities related to the finance world. Access to these local and regional professionals is a primary benefit of belonging to the UFO. In addition to the opportunity to meet and learn from these professionals, many members network and obtain internship or job opportunities from these events. The major benefit, however, is the annual trip to New York City. Members must be in good standing to be eligible to attend the yearly trip.

Members are the lifeblood of the UFO. Dues are relatively inexpensive, $25, and expectations are minimal. Members pay dues and attend meetings. A member in good standing is a student who pays dues and attends at least four of the weekly meetings each semester. Approximately eighty students are listed as members in good standing.

The UFO is led by the president, Jose, who is a full-time student. The president coordinates the speaker events and organizes the annual trip. Although supporting roles in the organization help the president accomplish these major goals, the president makes the key decisions and decides which responsibilities to delegate. To ensure that club activities are properly executed, effective delegation is essential. With weekly events, there is clearly too much for the president to do alone.

One of the primary challenges for the president is encouraging members to participate. Since Yvonne joined, she had attended almost every meeting. At these meetings, the highest level of attendance had been fifteen people. Yvonne felt that at less than 20 percent of the membership, this participation rate was low and a little embarrassing for the UFO. For the speakers, an audience of fifteen people can hardly seem worth their time. Yvonne felt that Jose was not effective at motivating members to attend the meetings more frequently.

Yvonne figured that if more members attended, the UFO could secure higher-quality speakers. She shared this idea with Jose, but he didn't feel he could do much more to get people to attend. He explained that he sent out emails every week to the membership list and had a calendar of speaker events posted by the student organization office. Jose commented that the incentive of participating in the yearly trip should be enough for members to meet the attendance requirement.

Now, Yvonne is considering the position of president for next year. The UFO is approaching its annual election of officers. Members have commented on a general lack of passion for the UFO. Yvonne comes to you to ask for your advice on the situation.

Questions:
1. What issues should Yvonne address to the members in relation to how they would benefit from her presidency?
2. What positions could the president create to help delegate the responsibilities associated with the UFO? How does delegation help a leader extend his or her influence?
3. What sorts of incentives might the UFO create to encourage higher participation rates?
4. What else can the UFO do as an organization to increase participation among its members?
5. What might Yvonne do to express her commitment to the organization? In what ways might her actions get others more excited about the UFO?

✦ Student Quotes

I like a leader who is compassionate, takes the project seriously, and has passion for what needs to be done.

I prefer a leader who is enthusiastic about his or her work and maintains a professional way of conducting themselves. Confidence is a great attribute in a leader.

If someone can tap into my emotions and get me motivated to believe what they do, I am more likely to follow.

I like for a leader to be honest with me, challenge me, and give me the needed support.

The leadership style which influences me is one where the leader is knowledgeable and confident, but the leader must also lead by example.

I need a leader who is empathetic to my situation and passionate about the cause in order to respect him.

When I see the leader doing their share of work, it motivates me to pull my own weight and do what I'm supposed to do.

If someone can keep my attention while providing me with a purpose then I will go with them until the project is complete. Direction and energy are what capture me.

ADDITIONAL RESOURCES

Bass, B. (1997). Does the transactional-transformational leadership paradigm transcend organizational and national boundaries? *American Psychology, 52*(2), 130–139.

Block, P. (1987). *The empowered manager: Positive political skills at work.* San Francisco: Jossey-Bass.

Daft, R. L. (2005). *The leadership experience* (3rd ed.). Canada: South-Western.

Goleman, D. (1995). *Emotional intelligence.* New York: Bantam Books.

Watkins, M. (2007). "Infectious leadership." The Leading Edge. Boston: Harvard Business Publishing. http://blogs.hbr.org/watkins/2007/10/infectious_leadership.html

19

Coaching

☚ Focus

Coaching entails helping others enhance their skills and abilities. Emotionally intelligent leaders know that they cannot do everything themselves. They need others to become a part of an endeavor. Coaching is about intentionally helping others demonstrate their talent and requires the emotionally intelligent leader to prioritize the time to foster the development of others in the group—not just themselves. Think about coaching as what you can do to help *train* and *prepare* another person. These words help connect coaching to emotionally intelligent leadership—doing what is necessary to help others for the challenges, tasks, or opportunities ahead. In a leadership context, coaching involves a willingness to learn from others. The relationship is reciprocal. One person does not know everything. Coaching others provides an easy vehicle for the learning to be shared and ideas to flow. At the heart of this capacity is the concept of developing others.

✦ Learning Objectives

- To develop communication and feedback skills
- To gain ideas from peers' feedback to improve leadership
- To apply the capacity of coaching as a way to enhance individual effectiveness

Coaching
Module 26, Activity 1: What Is Feedback?

By Darin Eich

Feedback calls for both awareness and creativity. The person offering feedback needs to be aware of when to offer the feedback, who is receiving the feedback, and the point of giving the feedback. At the same time, feedback should be offered in a way that it can be heard and applied—this often requires creativity.

What if we were to grade the feedback given to a person on a scale from A Level (highest quality, most helpful feedback) to F Level (useless, demeaning feedback)? What does each kind of feedback look like? Describe these here:

A Level

B Level

C Level

D Level

F Level

Coaching
Module 26, Activity 2: Feedback Assessment

By Darin Eich

This form can be used to share feedback. Share this document with someone so that she or he can give you feedback. Or, try this approach with someone to whom you need to give feedback.

This coaching is for _____.

When was this feedback offered? What was the setting? The situation?

Consider successes, strengths, opportunities, and ideas.

1. What was done well? What small or large successes occurred?

2. What strengths of the individual did you notice that he or she can continue to use and build on?

3. What opportunities exist for development to the next level?

Other comments:

← **Student Quotes**

I was supposed to deliver "bad" news to a group of students that I was co-leading. A project they had been working on was a "no-go" because of technicalities that were not addressed. It was the first time I was not going to be their "friend" anymore, but their leader instead. The woman who was our advisor talked to us about how to approach them . . . She was great about addressing any insecurities I had and helped me realize that it was not a personal issue, but a professional one.

For an entire year I led project meetings for an organization I was in. During this time I had a mentor who met weekly with me to discuss how the meeting went and what to do the following week. These meetings allowed my mentor to share with me their feelings about how the structure and flow of the meeting affected others.

As a freshman in high school, I gave a formal speech when running for a student council position. My friends taught me that such an address was not appropriate for that audience and I had to find other ways of earning the students' respect.

I meet with my advisor every Monday. We reflect on incidents that occurred throughout the week. I have had him remind me to keep my tone in check when talking to students so I do not let aggravation or frustration show. That is one thing that is hard to control when it shows in your voice *and* body language.

A fellow section member in wind symphony meets with me once a week to play duets to help me develop musically.

The first publisher I worked for often gave me tips and advice on how to improve my writing skills. He did so in a way that made me believe he was interested in my self-improvement as well as my ability to produce a better product for him. He never made me feel incompetent.

ADDITIONAL RESOURCES

Cook, M. J. (1998). *Effective coaching.* New York: McGraw Hill.

Cowan, S. L. (2006). *Seven keys for coaching power.* Amherst, MA: HRD Press.

Maxwell, J. C. (2008). *Mentoring 101.* Nashville, TN: Thomas Nelson.

Zachary, L. J. (2000). *The mentor's guide: Facilitating effective learning relationships.* San Francisco: Jossey-Bass.

20

Change Agent

↤ Focus

Being a change agent means you seek out and work with others toward new directions. As change agents, emotionally intelligent leaders look for opportunities for improvement or innovation—they think about possibilities and are future oriented. They see how change may benefit one person, an organization, or a whole community, and work to make this change happen. To be a change agent, you must possess certain skills, such as creative thinking and problem solving. In addition, you must have certain attitudes; for example, a comfort with risk taking and a desire to challenge the status quo. A change agent recognizes the importance of time. For change to be effective, you must consider the timing of a change effort and establish the appropriate level of urgency, knowing when to initiate a change and when to hold back.

✦ Learning Objectives

- To explore models of organizational change
- To design strategies to create effective change within an organization
- To reflect on a desired area in which you would like to initiate a change
- To practice creative problem-solving skills

Change Agent
Module 27, Activity 1: Current State of Organization

By Les Cook

If you were to imagine the ideal for

_____

(insert name of group/organization), what would it look like five years from now? Ten years?

Re-read the definition of change agent and answer the following: How can you be an agent of change?

Change Agent
Module 27, Activity 2: Driving Forces for Change

By Les Cook

Every organization or group experiences multiple influences from both within and outside its boundaries. Some of these forces are encouraging change (driving forces); others are resisting change (restraining forces). Some of these forces can be initiated or halted; others will continue regardless of what anyone does. Some of these forces are positive, others are not.

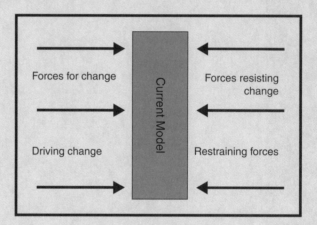

Provide the name of an organization or group you care about or are involved in:_____

List all the positive forces (for example, people, traditions, culture, external forces) that drive your organization toward evolving into a desired state; list all the constraining forces that are holding your organization back from evolving into a desired state.

Circle the forces that are critical to the future success of the organization or group.

Place a box around the forces that can be changed or influenced. Underline those that are out of your control.

Evaluate the strength of each force by placing a number next to it. (1 = weak; 10 = strong).

Change Agent
Module 28, Activity 2: Envision a Future

By Gabrielle Lucke

What do you really care about? Write down as many groups, issues, causes, and/or communities as you can think of that are important to you—so important that you would choose to devote your spare time to making them better.

Choose one item from this list and think about how you would describe its ideal future. What would the ideal future would look like? What would be happening? Who is involved? What are the positive experiences or outcomes that you hope for?

What steps could you take to make this happen?

What's stopping you?

✦ Student Quotes

We need people to pull ideas together to create change. A group is much more influential than an individual.

Leadership, put simply, changes things. . . such as taking initiative, balance, enthusiasm, communication—these can be used to improve organizations.

People must be involved to make changes within an organization. For these changes to be effective there must be a united front regarding the direction of the change, and this united front cannot form unless a leader (whether active or passive) is there to guide the discussion and actions of the group.

Change does not evolve without leadership, as fire cannot spread if no one strikes the match to start it.

There needs to be the catalyst for change, and sometimes it is someone who says, "Let's do this" that initiates that change. Change can be scary, but when someone gets momentum going, it is not so bad.

If there were no leaders to initiate change, we would live in a stagnant world.

ADDITIONAL RESOURCES

Books

Cramer, K., & Wasiak, H. (2006). *Change the way you see everything.* Philadelphia: Running Press.

Gardner, H. (2006). *Changing minds: The art and science of changing our own and other people's minds.* Cambridge, MA: Harvard Business School Press.

Peale, N. V. (2003). *The power of positive thinking.* New York: Fireside Books. (Original work published 1952)

Shankman, M. L., & Allen, S. J. (2008). *Emotionally intelligent leadership: A guide for college students.* San Francisco: Jossey-Bass.

Zander, R. S., & Zander, B. (2000). *The art of possibility: Transforming professional and personal life.* New York: Penguin Books.

Movies

Avatar (2009)

Hoot (2006)

Erin Brockovich (2000)

21

Conflict Management

⇜ Focus

Conflict management is about identifying and resolving problems and issues with others. Emotionally intelligent leaders
understand that conflict is part of any leadership experience.
When managed effectively, conflict can foster great innovation.
At times conflict is overt and may involve anger, raised voices,
or high levels of frustration. Other times conflict is below the
surface and shows itself only through cliques, side conversations,
and apathy. Emotionally intelligent leaders are aware of these
dynamics and work to manage them.

⇜ Learning Objectives

- To explore connections between honesty and conflict
- To identify the quality of personal and organizational inter-
  actions as they relate to conflict management
- To identify the roots of conflict
- To learn strategies for managing conflict

Conflict Management
Module 29: Honesty Article

By Mary Peterson

Almost any difficulty will move in the face of honesty.
When I am honest I never feel stupid.
And when I am honest I am automatically humble.
—Hugh Prather, *I Touch the Earth, the Earth Touches Me*

Webster's New Collegiate Dictionary defines *honest* as

1 (a) free from fraud or deception; legitimate, truthful (b) genuine, real (c) humble; 2 (a) reputable, respectful (b) good, worthy; 3—credible, praiseworthy; 4 (a) marked by integrity (b) frank, sincere (c) innocent, simple.

The *American Heritage College Dictionary* defines dialogue as 1—a conversation between two or more people; 5—an exchange of ideas or opinions.

Why use two different dictionary sources? To ensure an honest exchange of ideas, of course. So, according to *The Modern Mary Peterson Dictionary,* the definition of an honest dialogue would be the combination of the two sources: *a legitimate, frank conversation with yourself or two or more people, in which ideas and opinions are shared to create good and worthy ideas of integrity."*

You may now be asking why a definition of honest dialogue would include a conversation with yourself as one of its possibilities. To have honest dialogue with others, you need to be free from fraud and deception of self (*Webster's* 1a). It begins with you.

The definition seems so straightforward and simple, but it is difficult for humans to achieve. In fact, we have even created levels of honesty. Most people would say they value honesty in themselves and in others with whom they interact. You may recall, in the movie *A Few Good Men,* when Jack Nicholson's character responds to the Tom Cruise character, who has demanded, "I want the truth." With an angry and strong intonation, Nicholson's character replies, "You want the truth? You can't handle the truth!"

In some sense, that exchange says it all. We fight against the very thing we cry out for. We humans sure are complicated.

Some people will tell you they are being as honest as they can. The key is "as they can." This takes us back to having an honest dialogue with ourselves before doing it with others. Some believe being honest means being rebellious or difficult. For example, at a planning meeting facilitated by a colleague, a participant spoke up, saying he did not like a particular activity they were being asked to do. He said he didn't understand why they were being asked to draw a picture of their vision for the organization. He apologized for being honest. Jeffrey replied, "Honesty is not rebellion."

Honesty isn't rebellion. The truth was, this man really *did* understand why we were doing the vision exercise. He was not being honest with himself about the fact that it was hard for him to think outside the box and be creative and visionary. In his mind that statement would have been admitting a weakness. However, after being given some support and encouragement, he did an excellent job with his vision picture.

If we could only get over being independent and become more *interdependent*. Feeling secure in asking for help, rather than struggling on our own or dismissing the activity or challenge, is a step toward honesty with you.

Conflict Management
Module 29, Activity 1: Honesty Continuum

By Mary Peterson

List at least three examples of times when you responded with the level of honesty suggested.

Then think about the eventual outcomes of your level of honesty; what actually happened?

When was I . . .

Completely Honest?   *Outcome(s)*

1.

2.

3.

Somewhat Honest?   *Outcome(s)*

1.

2.

3.

Somewhat Dishonest?   *Outcome(s)*

1.

2.

3.

Completely Dishonest?   *Outcome(s)*

1.

2.

3.

Conflict Management
Module 29, Activity 2: Personal Interactions
Assessment

By Mary Peterson

To what extent do you agree or disagree with the following statements? Use the scale and place your ranking next to the number for each statement. Next, explain why you chose that ranking. In your responses, be consistent about the aspect of yourself that you are assessing (for example, as a formal leader or as a member of an organization or group).

Agree	Somewhat Agree	Somewhat Disagree	Disagree
4	3	2	1

___1. I am totally honest in all I have to say.
  Why?

___2. I prefer taking the time to understand others' points of view rather than to convince people of my own views.
  Why?

___3. I frequently ask people questions about their views.
Why?

___4. I think a lot about the differences in thinking that lead to conflict among people.
Why?

___5. I often change my ideas as a result of conversing with others.
Why?

Conflict Management
Module 29, Activity 3: Organizational Interactions Assessment

By Mary Peterson

To what extent do you agree or disagree with the following statements? Using the following scale, place your ranking next to each statement number and explain why you chose that ranking.

Agree	Somewhat Agree	Somewhat Disagree	Disagree
4	3	2	1

___1. My organization encourages people to take the time to communicate openly, even about difficult issues.
Why?

___2. My organization provides training and development for the skills needed to engage in constructive conflict.
Why?

___3. People respect different viewpoints and individual differences.
Why?

___4. Dissent and questioning are encouraged.
Why?

Conflict Management
Module 30, Activity 4: Basic Organizational Audit

By Michael Hayes

Think about an organization/group that you are a member of.

* How do members approach conflict? What are the cultural norms? Avoid? Confront? Collaborate?

* Where are you succeeding? Where are you failing?

* Is conflict a by-product of what's happening in your organization/group? If so, in what ways?

* What needs to change for your organization to work through conflict more effectively?

Conflict Management
Module 30, Activity 5: Scenarios

By Michael Hayes

Confrontation Model

1. Initiate contact.
2. Establish rapport.
3. Identify the issue or problem.
4. Agree on the problem.
5. Obtain a commitment.
6. Offer support on keeping the commitment.
7. Praise success!

Using this confrontation model, consider the following three scenarios. What would you do? Answer the questions that follow each of the scenarios.

Scenario One: A committee chair has failed to perform his or her duties on an important committee.

- What do you need to do to communicate honestly?

- How will you be sure to listen to all perspectives?

- What skills will you need to use to summarize all perspectives?

- What will you do to find common ground?

(Continued)

- How do you envision a decision getting made? Who's involved? How?

Scenario Two: A senior member has stopped attending meetings, and the member's historical perspective of your organization is missed.

- What do you need to do to communicate honestly?

- How will you be sure to listen to all perspectives?

- What skills will you need to use to summarize all perspectives?

- What will you do to find common ground?

- How do you envision a decision getting made? Who's involved? How?

Scenario Three: A friend has cheated on a recent exam or taken credit for work performed by someone else.

- What do you need to do to communicate honestly?

• How will you be sure to listen to all perspectives?

• What skills will you need to use to summarize all perspectives?

• What will you do to find common ground?

• How do you envision a decision getting made? Who's involved? How?

Source: Adapted from Shankman and Allen (2008).

← **Case Study: Tina's Planning Tragedy**

Amy Gourniak

The resident assistant office buzzed with excitement as the time drew near for the annual freshman residence hall formal. This year's event was sure to be a success, given the increase in the number of residents and a more enthusiastic staff of resident assistants (RAs). The RAs, who are all students working part-time in the residence halls, agreed that this time around, the formal would be the top Residence Life Department program by including both educational and entertainment elements. This would help fulfill the mission of both the department and the university: developing and nurturing students to become contributing citizens.

Tina had been on staff for three years and is the senior resident assistant (SRA), meaning she supervised a large number of RAs. She also served as the primary go-to person for the staff for the event. This was great for her, because she was particularly fond of the event. Tina believed strongly in the mission of the department and the university. She consistently searched for ways to tie their overarching principles into every aspect of her position, right down to the simplest "How are you doing?" conversation with one of her residents. She was proud that she was now able to inspire her fellow staff members to see ways in which the seemingly lofty goals could be included in an event like a student dance. As the staff-elected chairperson for the formal, Tina was confident that all the elements surrounding the event would come together exactly the way she wanted: perfectly.

Tina scheduled a meeting with her staff to start brainstorming for the event, including developing an outline of tasks and responsibilities. Though Tina made it clear to her staff members that it was not necessary to prepare anything for the meeting, she couldn't help but continue to plan and take note of any ideas that developed from her excitement over the event. By the night of the brainstorming meeting, Tina was proud that she had done her staff members the favor of thinking through every aspect of the event down to the finest detail. She figured this would help her staff so they wouldn't stress over how to make her grand vision a reality. By presenting her ideas, she assumed the staff would be able to spend their time energizing their residents and carrying out the tasks that Tina assigned.

The meeting unfolded with Tina leading the way. After a few cursory comments and introductory remarks, here's what transpired:

Tina: OK now, Mike, I want you to do the advertising—you're so good with the computer, so I know you'll make the best fliers around. Here is a sketch of what would make a great advertisement, and I've included five different themes and sayings to carry throughout the different ads. They're just the first things I could come up with off the top of my head, so feel free to adjust as you see fit.

Mike: Um, OK, Tina, but I'm not very good at the design element. Jess is the artistic one—can I have her help me design the ads?

Tina: Well, no, because I need Jess to help me with the decorations. Don't doubt your abilities, Mike. I've sketched the whole thing out for you, anyway. You'll be fine! Now, Jess, as I mentioned, I thought you would be great at decorating the facility.

Jess: Oh, that's awesome, Tina! I'm picturing pink tassels to accentuate green ribbons to hang from the door . . .

Tina: [*interrupting with a nervous laugh*] Well, Jess, those sound like great ideas, but I'm not quite sure if they will fit with the overall theme of the event. Take a look at the notes I've made here for you regarding the thematic elements of the formal. I've concluded that blues and yellows will be more appropriate. I thought about it for a long time, but if you'd like to consider something different, let me know. Yet, I'd hate for you to spend the time rethinking what I've already thought about when you could be spending your time getting started, don't you agree?

Jess: [*silent pause*] I guess so. I'll get started, but maybe think about it some more as I go.

Tina: Suit yourself, but make sure you realize that the first few items on my list take three weeks to arrive, so they'll need to be ordered pretty soon.

Tina continued to divide the tasks she had created in the same manner. She based her decisions on what she knew about her staff members' skills and interests. Tina set the deadlines, the team agreed, and then everyone dispersed to their respective hallways to begin their assignments.

Tina felt energized. She couldn't help but think, however, that her staff members weren't as excited as she was. Tina brushed off this notion, trusting that the tasks she had given the RAs would excite them. Soon enough, her staff would see her vision and become more enthusiastic given their realized individual importance in making the event a reality. Or so Tina thought . . .

As the first round of deadlines approached, Tina called another staff meeting. She was excited to see the work her team members accomplished. She asked each staff member to share his or her progress with the group. However, Tina's excitement turned to anxiety as she saw less and less of what she had envisioned.

Tina: But, Mike, those fliers look nothing like my sketch. You did a really great job, but it's just not what I expected. I'll simply redo them for you. Will you at least still take them to the printer?

Mike: Yeah, I guess. Sorry, Tina.

Tina: Oh, don't worry about it! I must not have been clear. So, Jess, how are the decorations coming along?

Jess: Great! I managed to find a different pink material that worked perfectly with your blues and can be delivered in half the time! I went ahead and ordered it, so what else can I help you with now?

Tina: Geez, Jess, I would've appreciated you running the order by me before you placed it, but I guess it's too late now. I'll take care of the rest of it. Don't worry about it. I don't want to stifle your creativity at all, so why don't you help Mike hang up the fliers when they're printed?

The meeting outcome was not what Tina had envisioned. Two other members of the staff hadn't followed through on their assignments at all, so Tina said she'd take care of those responsibilities. Two RAs even got into an argument about the music, even though Tina had already announced what the lineup would be. In the end, the staff left the meeting grumbling and unenthusiastic about the next step.

As Tina walked back to her room, she felt overwhelmed with the large number of tasks she now had to accomplish by herself. She couldn't help but think, "Why couldn't my staff just do what they were supposed to? I had it all planned perfectly, and now I have to redo everything I already spent the time to plan the event right the first time!" Tina felt frustrated, stressed, and deflated—and she couldn't figure out why her staff felt the same way.

Questions:
1. If the scenario continues as described, how successful will Tina and her staff be in coordinating the residence hall formal? How might the dynamics of the group change throughout the process?

2. What specific actions did Tina take that led to her staff's lack of enthusiasm?

3. Would you describe this scenario as one in which conflict is present? If so, in what ways? If not, why not?

4. How could Tina have incorporated her team in different ways to create more synergy?

5. What can Tina do or how can Tina change to become a stronger leader? How might she employ one of the models for managing conflict?

← Student Quotes

You must utilize all of the resources of each member of the team. When a person has something to offer and feels that his/her assets are not being utilized, they will become disengaged. Conflict management works the same way. You must first acknowledge the mutual worth of each member, maintaining a positive attitude and acknowledging faults on both sides. At that point you can then start working toward a solution.

You must decipher the problem and come up with a plan of attack. Cooperation and communication skills are a necessity.

To be effective at managing conflict, one must be neutral and willing to hear both sides of the story. I have experienced this through peer mediation. It's difficult at times; however, I know that there must be common ground to resolve conflict.

There was a roommate conflict and one roommate wanted to move out. That roommate approached me and we decided to have a discussion with our other roommate. The open communication among the three of us was very important to getting to the root of the problem. The ability to compromise was essential to coming up with a solution.

People often argue on policies and rules. When people are in conflict it takes a mediator who is unbiased and calm and will present each side in a different light.

At my job my co-workers and I needed to come up with a solution . . . To manage conflict you must be smart, compromise, and think critically and keep in mind the final objective.

ADDITIONAL RESOURCES

Bolton, R. (1979). *People skills: How to assert yourself, listen to others and resolve conflicts.* New York: Simon & Schuster.

Fisher, R., & Shapiro, D. (2006). *Beyond reason: Using emotions as you negotiate.* New York: Penguin.

Patterson, K., Grenny, J., McMillan, R., & Switzler, A. (2002). *Crucial conversations: Tools for talking when stakes are high.* New York: McGraw-Hill.

Scott, S. (2002). *Fierce conversations: Achieving success at work and life one conversation at a time.* New York: Berkley Books.

22

Developing Relationships

✦ Focus

Developing relationships is about creating connections between, among, and with people. It is a skill as well as a mindset. This capacity requires emotionally intelligent leaders to build relationships and create a sense of trust and mutual interest. Simply put, individuals, groups, and organizations are stronger, smarter, and more effective when they are rooted in and facilitate positive relationships. Some people assume you have to be outgoing or social to be effective at developing relationships; however, networking experts have discovered that the people who are best at developing relationships are not necessarily gregarious. They possess a combination of skills and the understanding that they need to listen well, know themselves, and know how to develop rapport with others. People who understand the valuable role that others play in making their own lives rich and fulfilling are often the best at developing relationships, regardless of personality type.

✦ Learning Objectives

- To learn about the benefits of and strategies for networking
- To identify important people with whom to connect
- To explore the dynamics of teamwork as a way to foster developing relationships

Developing Relationships
Module 31, Activity 1: Personal Networking Web

By Paige Haber

Think about the people and organizations that provide you with opportunities to grow (for example, friends, family, employers, mentors, coaches, supervisors, pastor, rabbi, alumni, current and former classmates). Identify the different networks and relationships in your life that can or will make a difference in who you become or what you do. Don't think too much about this. If a person's name or the name of an organization comes up, go with it. Write it down and draw a line to your circle. If there are connections between the different individuals or groups that you think of, feel free to draw connecting lines between them.

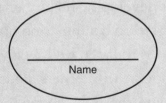

Name

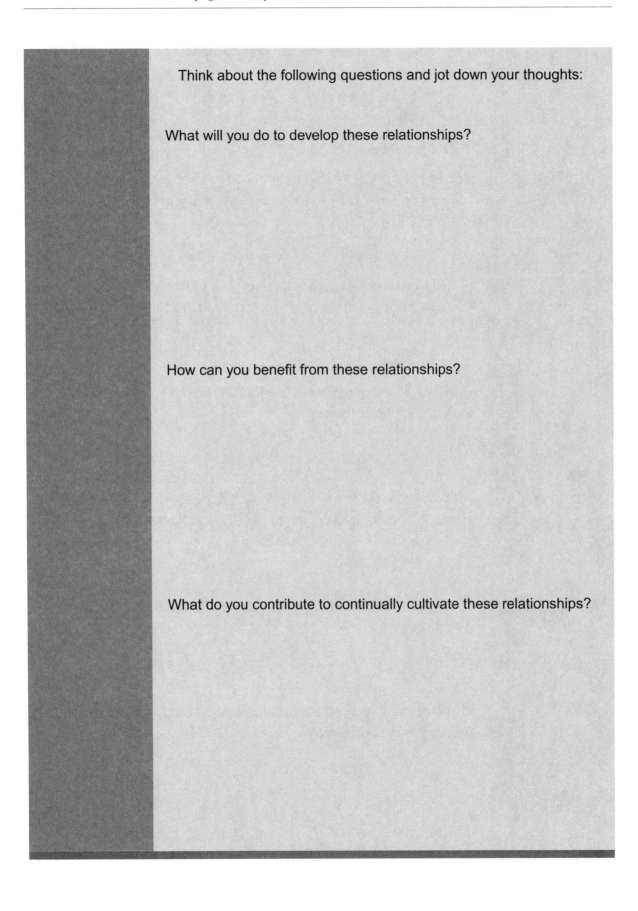

Think about the following questions and jot down your thoughts:

What will you do to develop these relationships?

How can you benefit from these relationships?

What do you contribute to continually cultivate these relationships?

Developing Relationships
Module 31, Activity 2: Personal Networking
Action Planning

By Paige Haber

Looking at Activity 1, what patterns do you see in your personal networking web? How would you describe any gaps that you see?

What opportunities do you see in your personal network web that you can use, personally or professionally, in the next three months?

What potential connections with your network can you facilitate for a friend or classmate?

What connections or relationships may require some additional attention or reconnection to maintain this relationship in the future?

How do you see your personal networking web changing in the next three years?

What steps can you take at this point in your life to expand your personal networking web?

✦ Case Study: Fostering Teamwork Through Developing Relationships

Mark Greisberger

It was a cold early Monday morning in late December when team captain Justin Credible walked into his high school gymnasium. Justin was now a senior, a three-year varsity athlete, and captain of the reigning New York State Division AA baseball team. Being captain earned him great respect, but with it came even more responsibility. His high school was a perennial powerhouse, and after winning the state title in the previous year, expectations were high. Based on his experience the previous year, Justin believed that team spirit and unity were its greatest strengths. Although the team had multiple coaches, the captain had the primary responsibility to build the team into a cohesive unit. Justin knew that establishing strong relationships among the players was the only means of accomplishing this goal.

The good news was that Justin was known as a team player. He was never late, was respectful of others, and compliant with the coaches and captains before him. He was comfortable as a follower; he enjoyed friendships with many different guys on the team and excelled at fitting in. This was one reason why he was elected team captain, but the role was a big change for him. Never before had he felt responsible for an entire group of people.

The best player on the team was a junior named Holden. Holden had great skills and knew it. He was also a bit of a prankster, so he presented both a great challenge and a potential asset to Justin. Justin's other big challenge was Coach Peterson; he was a demanding coach, driven by results (not excuses). He held his players to a high standard and expected great effort all the time. He had little patience for anyone's inability to complete the job at a high level.

Throughout the season, Justin often struggled with maintaining his responsibility as the captain. Some portions of the job came easily to him. For example, leading by example was natural for Justin. He was the first to show up and the last to leave; he ran out every ground ball, cheered for his teammates, and played hard. However, Justin struggled to foster the same mindset in his teammates. Players consistently showed up late to early morning practices and often skipped team events such as meetings and dinners. The team was also divided into two factions—one of them led by Holden.

Coach Peterson expressed his unhappiness about the team's behavior to Justin, since he was responsible for it. Justin thought he had done a good job of talking with his teammates, but he realized he hadn't been successful at bringing his team together and meeting Coach's high standard. Coach expected the team to develop a strong sense of camaraderie. Justin needed to facilitate change, but he couldn't figure out how. He knew just one thing—Holden held the key.

Questions:

1. What should Justin's first step be?
2. How can Justin work effectively with Holden? What should Justin do to make this happen?
3. In what ways can Justin use the respect the team has for him to improve relationships on the team?
4. Why does Coach Peterson hold Justin personally responsible for the faults of others on the team?
5. In what ways are relationships among teammates a crucial element to this story? In what other situations might the relationships among group members have greater importance than the skills or talents present?

❧ Student Quotes

To build new relationships, I normally start by watching the person's interactions with other people. Then I try to interact with them in a friendly manner.

It is critical to ask questions and listen. By asking questions and carefully listening, an individual can quickly find out another's interests, passions, and feelings. This simple process is the beginning to building new relationships.

To build a relationship, I simply start by talking to people about things that we have in common such as work or classes. For me in particular this is hard. I feel that I am a shy person around people I don't know well.

To build new relationships I simply speak up and ask questions with sincerity.

Relationships are formed through trust, and knowing the individual. You must understand someone and relate to their situation.

ADDITIONAL RESOURCES

Bacharach, S. B. (2005). *Get them on your side*. Avon, MA: Platinum Press.

Brown, J., Isaacs, D., & the World Café Community. (2005). *The world café: Shaping our futures through conversations that matter*. San Francisco: Berrett-Koehler.

Carnegie, D. (1998). *How to win friends and influence people*. New York: Pocket. (Originally published in 1936)

Wheatley, M. (2002). *Turning to one another: Simple conversations to restore hope to the future*. San Francisco: Berrett-Koehler.

23

Teamwork

⤺ Focus

Teamwork is about working effectively with others in a group. Emotionally intelligent leaders know how to work with others to bring out the best in each team member. By facilitating good communication, creating shared purpose, clarifying roles, and facilitating results, emotionally intelligent leaders foster group cohesion and truly develop a sense of togetherness that leads to desired results. Teamwork is about knowing when to assert and when to hold back. Many leadership experts propose that sometimes the most influential act of leadership is to take a step back and follow. When you know how to work well with others, you create an environment where working together is expected.

⤺ Learning Objectives

- To articulate personal perspectives on teamwork
- To explore different definitions of teamwork
- To identify a personal commitment to enhance collaboration skills

Teamwork
Module 33, Activity 1: Visualizing Teamwork

By Karyn Nishimura Sneath

On a blank sheet of paper, create a visual representation of specific phrases or images which convey their assumptions about teamwork. Cut out phrases, words, pictures, and so on from magazines or newspapers. Feel free to use your own artistic skills and draw your thoughts.

If it helps, think about what is important to you as you work in a team.

Describe how this representation helps you think about:

- Your assumptions and/or expectations about being part of a team

- Some lessons to keep in mind as you work to strengthen a team or set of relationships

- Your commitments to others as you focus on collaboration and team contributions

✦ Case Study: The Captain, For Better or Worse

John Smith

In recent years, High Point College benefited from a good, though not great men's basketball team. The team steadily improved its record, and more fans came to the games each season. Last year the team consisted of twelve players, but only eight of them saw real playing time. The other four players practiced regularly, but the coach was not convinced they were prepared for actual competition.

This past year only two seniors were on the team. The star of the team, Joe, was one of the seniors and served as the captain. The team looked up to Joe for his expertise and knowledge of the game. He was a four-year starter who averaged twenty-one points and seven assists per game. He had great leadership skills that showed in the way that he worked well with his teammates, inspired others to do their best, and had a drive to win that was contagious. He struggled, however, with controlling his emotions.

Joe's skills on the court impressed his teammates and coaches. He was not a selfish player. He knew he could do it all, but he wanted to get his teammates involved. As a leader, Joe was close with his teammates, and they shared the same goal of trying to win each game.

The two other skilled players on the team were a sophomore named Brian and a junior named Chris. Brian was a great three-point shooter; Chris was a post player who averaged eleven rebounds a game.

These three players played virtually every minute of every game; they were the heart and soul of the team. Even though Brian and Chris were good players, they looked up to Joe as their leader. Although strong on the court, Brian and Chris were followers and waited for Joe to take the lead. In essence, they lacked many of the qualities needed to be a leader on the team.

Joe faced many challenges with his lack of emotional self-control. Joe let his emotions get the best of him during games. When calls didn't go his way or if he wasn't making shots, he would lose his temper. In many games he would get a technical foul for complaining with the referees or yelling after a bad play. Some of these technical fouls came at key moments and cost the team the game.

Joe also took out his anger on his teammates. For instance, when they would miss shots or turn the ball over, he got frustrated with them for making mistakes. He often yelled at them and criticized them, even during the games themselves. Joe also struggled when his coach pulled him out of the game. It seemed to Joe that each time this happened, the team fell apart without him—their leader—in the game. Sometimes Joe would get so mad for being benched that he argued with the coach. This behavior got Joe (and the team) nowhere.

During practices Joe worked with his teammates to try to help them out, almost like an assistant coach. But Joe felt that because he was the best player and had seniority on the team, he didn't have to practice as hard as the rest or do everything the others did. Joe argued with the coach when the coach challenged him to be an equal member of the team and practice hard like the rest of them. The team felt let down by Joe's anger and lack of respect for the coach. In the heat of the moment, Joe didn't know he was offending his teammates by getting upset and showing his emotions. Joe did not realize that his full effort in practice would help his team as a whole. Even if he didn't need the practice every day, the team needed him there and needed his constant leadership. Unfortunately, Joe didn't fully appreciate how the team needed him.

Questions:

1. In what ways did Joe positively impact the quality of the team? How did he negatively affect the team?

2. What could the coach have done differently in dealing with a player like Joe?
3. How might Joe's teammates have helped Joe better appreciate the role that he played on the team?
4. What would you suggest to Joe to help him improve his role on the team?
5. How might this situation be different if Joe were not one of the best players on the team?

⬥ Student Quotes

For a team to succeed, there must be dedication and commitment to the task at hand. Without direction, the team won't do well.

[For a team to succeed] members must be open to a possibilities different from their own.

People must understand that each member has valuable input for the group. It is also important for the team to not come to decisions too quickly or too slowly. It is important to examine numerous possibilities to ensure that the action taken is one of the best options. A team must believe in each of its members, and every member must contribute for a team to succeed.

If you have one person who doesn't care, it can bring down the morale of the entire team. Everyone should respect each other's thought and opinions, even if they do not share them.

I work in an accounting department for an organization and every day we work in groups. Information is passed from one person to another. Without this passing of information, there would be no business. I have also discovered that for this to succeed there must be an open line of communication.

To work as one, there must be an understanding of peace and knowing that each has their opinion and that they have the right to voice it. Also there must be an agreement that there are responsibilities involved that must be fulfilled to succeed. Factors that need to be present are flexibility, respect, and understanding.

The real key to a successful team is having a firm understanding of the goal of the group, and then knowing how each individual can most effectively contribute to the achievement of this goal.

ADDITIONAL RESOURCES

Books

Avery, C. M., Walker, M. A., & O'Toole, E. (2001). *Teamwork is an individual skill: Getting your work done when sharing responsibility.* San Francisco: Berrett-Koehler.

Katzenbach, J. R., & Smith, D. K. (1993). *The wisdom of teams: Creating the high-performance organization.* New York: HarperBusiness.

Larson, C. E., & LaFasto, F.M.J. (1989). *Teamwork: What must go right/what can go wrong.* Newbury Park, CA: Sage.

Lencioni, P. (2002). *The five dysfunctions of a team: A leadership fable.* San Francisco: Jossey-Bass.

Movies

The Blind Side (2009)

Glory Road (2006)

Ratatouille (2007)

24

Capitalizing on Difference

Focus

Capitalizing on difference is about building on assets that stem from differences between people. Capitalizing on difference suggests that differences are seen as assets, not barriers. Difference may mean race, socio-economic status, religion, sexual orientation, or gender, as well as ability, personality, or philosophy. When capitalized on, these differences create a larger perspective—a more inclusive view. Emotionally intelligent leaders use these differences as an opportunity to help others grow, develop, and ultimately build on them. Whatever they may be, you have the capacity to learn about these differences. When you capitalize on these assets, you understand the power that can be drawn from a wider perspective, set of ideas, talents, or world views. To capitalize on difference, you must possess a desire to learn, have an open mind, and be willing to change your mind. Doing this can be challenging—and also rewarding for you, the people with whom you interact, and the cause or organization that you serve.

✦ Learning Objectives

- To explore the concepts of social identity and privilege
- To learn how multiple perspectives influence your perceptions
- To reflect on the multiple identities with which you identify
- To explore the concept of what an inclusive campus/ organization looks like

Capitalizing on Difference
Module 34, Activity 1: The Diversity Wheel

By Tara Edberg

Diversity refers to the multifaceted ways in which human beings can be both similar and different. The Diversity Wheel model illustrates the primary and secondary dimensions of diversity that exert an effect on each of us at home, at work, and in society. Although each dimension adds a layer of complexity to individual identity, it is the dynamic interaction among all the dimensions that influences self-image, values, opportunities, and expectations. Together, the primary and secondary dimensions of diversity give definition and meaning to our lives by contributing to a synergistic, integrated whole—the diverse person. *Circle the dimensions that relate to you.*

Primary Dimensions

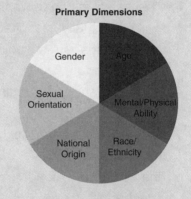

Secondary Dimensions

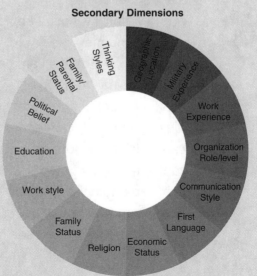

Source: Tara Edberg, referenced from *Implementing Diversity* © 1996. Irwin Professional Publishing.

Capitalizing on Difference
Module 34, Activity 2: Privilege Statements

By Tara Edberg

Consider the following:

> I have come to see privilege as an invisible package of unearned assets that I can count on cashing in each day, but about which I was "meant" to remain oblivious. Privilege is like an invisible weightless knapsack of special provisions, maps, passports, codebooks, visas, clothes, tools, and blank checks. (McIntosh, 1999, p. 1)

With this definition in mind, circle up to ten statements that you believe are true for you.

1. I make a dollar to every seventy-eight cents a woman makes.
2. I feel safe walking down the street at night without a fear that I will be sexually assaulted or raped.
3. I can speak about my political beliefs without being considered overly religious.
4. When I go shopping, I can do so without being followed or harassed.
5. When I am out in public, I do not have to worry that people may think I am a terrorist.
6. The academic calendar revolves around my religious calendar/holidays.
7. When I watch TV, I see people of my race widely represented in a positive manner.
8. I believe no one thinks I am unhealthy, unfit, or unemployable because of my body type.
9. I can be reasonably sure that when I wear a symbol of my religion, people do not fear me.
10. I can criticize my government without being seen as an outsider.
11. I can be talkative or moody without it being attributed to my gender.
12. I can slap another man's rear end after a football game and say "Good Game" without it being attributed to my sexuality.
13. I can turn on the TV and see family units similar to mine depicted positively on TV.

14. I have traveled to other countries and toured several states in the US.

15. When I testify in a court of law, I am sworn in on my religion's holy book.

16. I can enter every building on campus without worrying about the route I take.

17. I am sure that no one thinks I am unintelligent because of my accent.

18. I can buy new clothes, go out to dinner or see a dentist, doctor, or lawyer when I need to.

Source: Adapted from McIntosh, P. M. (1989, July-August). White privilege: Unpacking the invisible knapsack. *Peace and Freedom*, 10–12.

Now consider the following questions:

• What are the social influences that affect your identity?

• Had you thought about this before? If so, what causes you to think about these things? If not, how will you think about this in the future?

• How does this knowledge of yourself influence your leadership?

• Do you know this information about people with whom you work? If so, how? If not, how might you learn it?

Capitalizing on Difference
Module 35, Activity 3: Braids of Multiple Identities

By Susana Muñoz

Individuals are composed of different identities. Consider the diagram:

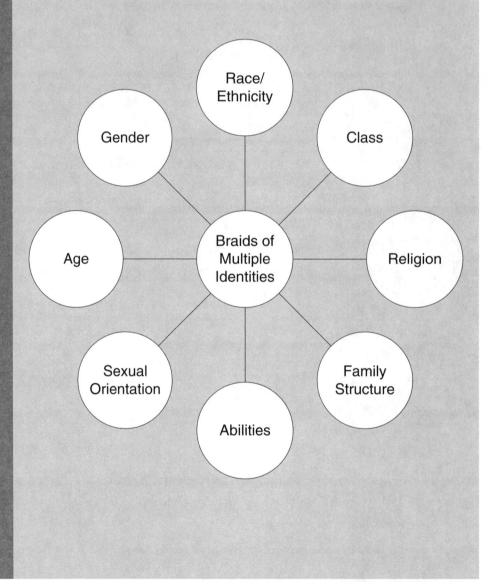

These are just some examples of different identities that individuals possess. From the identities shown, choose three that reflect the most influential aspects of who you are, or write your own. The point is to identify the most influential aspects of who you are.

1.

2.

3.

What do your multiple identities mean for you as a leader?

When or how are your multiple identities validated or invalidated?

Capitalizing on Difference
Module 35, Activity 4: Action Planning

By Susana Muñoz

Action Planning

To create a more inclusive campus/organization, what can we:

Start doing?

Stop doing?

Continue doing?

← Student Quotes

Different cultural and social backgrounds can be both beneficial and non-beneficial. It depends on the maturity of the persons working together. If they respect each other, people from different backgrounds could develop some great ideas.

Diversity inspires creativity. It is the driving force behind innovation and collaboration.

Different people bring different ideas, and when they are allowed to grow in a respectful atmosphere, the results can be fantastic.

Every individual brings a different background to the table even if they were raised in a similar culture. When culture, politics, and philosophy are brought into the mix, the original means of leadership may be challenged and in the end changed.

Differences bring out varying viewpoints and a wider range of ideas, but can also lead to contention. A common goal may be harder to reach.

Differences allow greater adaptability and versatility for solving problems and communicating with other groups; however, they are an opportunity for conflict. Whether it is a good or bad thing depends on the surrounding circumstances.

ADDITIONAL RESOURCES

Books

Gallagher Hateley, B. J., & Schmidt, W. H. (2001). *A peacock in the land of penguins: A fable about creativity and courage.* San Francisco: Berrett-Koehler.

Peterson, B. (2004). *Cultural intelligence: A guide to working with people from other cultures.* Yarmouth, ME: Intercultural Press.

Raines, C. (2003). *Connecting generations: The sourcebook for a new workplace.* Menlo Park, CA: Crisp Publications.

Silberman, M., & Hansburg, F. (2000). *PeopleSmart: Developing your interpersonal intelligence.* San Francisco: Berrett-Koehler.

Movies

Avatar (2010)

Crash (2005)

Dead Poets Society (1989)

Glory Road (2006)

Leadership is available to all of us. In fact, you do not need a formal title or position to lead others (think of Gandhi and Martin Luther King, Jr.). Sometimes you make a conscious decision to pursue a leadership role; other times the opportunity simply presents itself and you "step up." Either way, we agree with Joseph Rost (1993), who suggests that leadership is "an influence relationship among leaders and followers who intend real changes that reflect their mutual purposes" (p. 102). In other words, leaders and followers often collaborate toward a common end point. Each of us, often in a moment's notice, move from leader to follower depending on the context. So we suggest that leaders and followers can behave in an emotionally intelligent manner—it's not just about emotionally intelligent leadership, it's about emotionally intelligent followership as well.

Emotionally intelligent leadership asserts that an individual must be conscious of three fundamental facets that contribute to the leadership dynamic: consciousness of context, of self, and of others. These three facets overlap yet are independent of each other. Each facet consists of specific capacities that can be developed. A person's ability to monitor all three facets intentionally will enhance the person's ability to lead effectively.

Consciousness of Context

- *Environmental awareness:* Thinking intentionally about the environment of a leadership situation. The larger system, or environment, directly influences an individual's ability to lead. Aspects of the environment affect the psychological and interpersonal dynamics of any human interaction. Emotionally intelligent leaders are in tune with a variety of factors such as community traditions and customs, the political environment, and major institutions (e.g., religion, government).

• *Group savvy*: Interpreting the situation and/or networks of an organization. Every group has written/unwritten rules, ways of operating, customs and rituals, power dynamics, internal politics, inherent values, and so forth. Emotionally intelligent leaders know how to diagnose and interpret these dynamics. Demonstrating group savvy enables one to have a direct influence on the work of the group.

Consciousness of Self

• *Emotional self-perception*: Identifying your emotions and reactions and their impact on you. Emotional self-perception means that individuals are acutely aware of their feelings (in real time). In addition, emotional self-perception means understanding how these feelings lead to behaviors. Having emotional self-perception also means that emotionally intelligent leaders have a choice as to how they respond. This capacity enables one to differentiate between the emotions felt and the actions taken. In most situations, both healthy and unhealthy responses are available.

• *Honest self-understanding*: Being aware of your own strengths and limitations. Honest self-understanding means that an individual celebrates and honors their strengths and talents while acknowledging and addressing limitations. Honest self-understanding means accepting the good and bad about one's personality, abilities, and ideas. When emotionally intelligent leaders demonstrate honest self-understanding, they embody a foundational capacity of effective leadership—the ability to see a more holistic self and understand how this impacts their leadership.

- *Healthy self-esteem:* Having a balanced sense of self. Emotionally intelligent leaders possess a high level of self-worth, are confident in their abilities, and are willing to stand up for what they believe in. They are also balanced by a sense of humility and the ability to create space for the opinions, perspectives, and thoughts of others.

- *Emotional self-control:* Consciously moderating your emotions and reactions. Although feeling emotions and being aware of them is part of this statement, so too is regulating them. Emotional self-control is about both awareness (being conscious of feelings) and action (managing emotions and knowing when and how to show them). Recognizing feelings, understanding how and when to demonstrate those feelings appropriately, and taking responsibility for one's emotions (versus being victims of them) are critical components of this capacity.

- *Authenticity:* Being transparent and trustworthy. Authenticity is a complex concept that emphasizes the importance of being trustworthy, transparent, and living in a way in which words match actions and vice versa. This is no small order. Being authentic means, in part, that emotionally intelligent leaders follow through on commitments and present themselves and their motives in an open and honest manner.

- *Flexibility:* Being open and adaptive to changing situations. The best laid plans don't always come to fruition, so emotionally intelligent leaders need to be responsive to change and open to feedback. By thinking creatively and using their problem-solving skills, emotionally intelligent leaders engage others in determining a new way to reach their goals.

- *Achievement:* Being driven to improve according to personal standards. An important nuance of this capacity is the role of personal standards. Individuals often know achievement when they see and feel it. Instead of letting others define what achievement looks like, emotionally intelligent leaders pursue their passions and goals to a self-determined level of accomplishment.

This drive produces results and may inspire others to become more focused in their efforts or to work at increased levels as well.

- *Optimism:* Being positive. Emotionally intelligent leaders demonstrate a healthy, positive outlook and display a positive regard for the future. Optimism is a powerful force that many overlook. When demonstrated effectively, optimism is contagious and spreads throughout a group or organization.

- *Initiative:* Wanting and seeking opportunities. Emotionally intelligent leaders understand and take initiative. This means being assertive and seeking out opportunities. Emotionally intelligent leaders have to both see the opportunity for change and make it happen. Demonstrating initiative means that individuals take action and help the work of the group move forward.

Consciousness of Others

- *Empathy:* Understanding others from their perspective. Emotionally intelligent leadership and, more specifically, the capacity of empathy are about perceiving the emotions of others. When leaders display empathy, they have the opportunity to build healthier relationships, manage difficult situations, and develop trust more effectively. Being empathetic requires an individual to have a high level of self-awareness as well as awareness of others.

- *Citizenship:* Recognizing and fulfilling your responsibility for others or the group. Emotionally intelligent leaders must be aware of what it means to be a part of something bigger than themselves. An essential component is to fulfill the ethical and moral obligations inherent in the values of the community. As a result, emotionally intelligent leaders know when to give of themselves for the benefit of others and the larger group.

- *Inspiration:* Motivating and moving others toward a shared vision. Being perceived as an inspirational individual by others is an important capacity of emotionally intelligent leadership.

Inspiration works through relationships. Effective leadership entails generating feelings of optimism and commitment to organizational goals through individual actions, words, and accomplishments.

- *Influence:* Demonstrating skills of persuasion. Emotionally intelligent leaders have the ability to persuade others with information, ideas, emotion, behavior, and a strong commitment to organizational values and purpose. They involve others to engage in a process of mutual exploration and action.

- *Coaching:* Helping others enhance their skills and abilities. Emotionally intelligent leaders know that they cannot do everything themselves. They need others to become a part of the endeavor. Coaching is about intentionally helping others demonstrate their talent and requires the emotionally intelligent leader to prioritize the time to foster the development of others in the group—not just themselves.

- *Change agent:* Seeking out and working with others toward new directions. As change agents, emotionally intelligent leaders look for opportunities for improvement or innovation— they think about possibilities and are future oriented. They see how change may benefit one person, an organization, or a whole community, and work to make this change happen.

- *Conflict management:* Identifying and resolving problems and issues with others. Emotionally intelligent leaders understand that conflict is part of any leadership experience. When managed effectively, conflict can foster great innovation. At times conflict is overt and may involve anger, raised voices, or high levels of frustration. Other times conflict is below the surface and shows itself only through cliques, side conversations, and apathy. Emotionally intelligent leaders are aware of these dynamics and work to manage them.

- *Developing relationships:* Creating connections between, among, and with people. Developing relationships is a skill as well as a mind-set. This capacity requires emotionally intelligent leaders to build relationships and create a sense of trust and mutual interest. Simply put, individuals, groups, and organizations are stronger, smarter, and more effective when they are rooted in and facilitate positive relationships.

- *Teamwork:* Working effectively with others in a group. Emotionally intelligent leaders know how to work with others to bring out the best in each team member. By facilitating good communication, creating shared purpose, clarifying roles, and facilitating results, emotionally intelligent leaders foster group cohesion and truly develop a sense of togetherness that leads to desired results.

- *Capitalizing on differences:* Building on assets that come from differences with others. Capitalizing on difference suggests that differences are seen as assets, not barriers. Difference may mean race, socio-economic status, religion, sexual orientation, or gender as well as ability, personality, or philosophy. When capitalized upon, these differences create a larger perspective—a more inclusive view. Emotionally intelligent leaders use these differences as an opportunity to help others grow, develop, and ultimately capitalize on them.

Where Emotional Intelligence and Student Leadership Unite

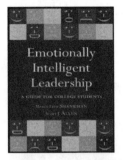

The book *Emotionally Intelligent Leadership* offers an in-depth explanation of the model and the tools for reflection on the concepts of leadership.

ISBN: 978-0-470-27713-3

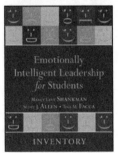

Emotionally Intelligent Leadership for Students—Inventory offers a formative learning experience. The *Inventory* is an opportunity for individuals to explore their experiences in leadership with a focus on learning one's strengths and limitations based on past behaviors.

ISBN: 978-0-470-61572-0

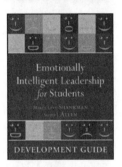

Emotionally Intelligent Leadership for Students—Development Guide offers further guidance for development for each of the 21 capacities, including: definitions, student quotes, suggested experiences and activities, further reading and films to watch, notable quotes, and reflection questions.

ISBN: 978-0-470-61573-7

Emotionally Intelligent Leadership for Students—Workbook brings further understanding and relevancy to the EILS model. It includes modularized learning activities for each capacity, as well as some case studies, and resources for additional learning. It can be used as part of a facilitated course or workshop, or as a stand-alone, follow-up experience that students can use on their own.

ISBN: 978-0-470-61574-4

Emotionally Intelligent Leadership for Students—Facilitation and Activity Guide uses step-by-step instructions to lead facilitators and instructors through modularized activities found in the *EILS Workbook*. The modularized, timed activities can be taught out of sequence and customized to fit the needs of a curricular or co-curricular program. The guide offers various options and scenarios for using activities in different settings with different time constraints.

ISBN: 978-0-470-61575-1

SAVE ON SETS

Sets tailored for facilitators and students are available at discounted prices.
Visit www.josseybass.com for more information

—